JESUITS AT AKBAR'S COURT

JESUITS AT AKBAR'S COURT

Christian Missionaries in Mughal India

YOURI MARTINI

MANOHAR
2025

Cover illustration: Jesus being portrayed by King Abgar's painter, from a *Mir'at al-quds* of Father Jerome Xavier (Spanish, 1549-1617), 1602-04. Mughal India, Allahabad, made for Prince Salim (1569-1627). Gum tempera, ink, and gold on paper; page: 26.2 × 15.6 cm (10 5/16 × 6 1/8 in.). The Cleveland Museum of Art, John L. Severance Fund 2005.145.143.a

First published 2025
First eBook edition 2025

ISBN 978-93-6080-097-0 (hardbound)
ISBN 978-93-6080-184-7 (eBook)

Published by
Ajay Kumar Jain *for*
Manohar Publishers & Distributors
4753/23 Ansari Road, Daryaganj
New Delhi 110002

Cover design by Kamal Purna Jammual

Typeset by Ravi Shanker, Delhi 110095

Printed and bound in India

To

PROFESSOR FRANCESCO SURDICH

&

PROFESSOR ALBERTO TORRESANI,

with heartfelt gratitude for their
guidance, inspiration, and academic support,
which have profoundly enriched my scholarly journey.

"*Extende caritatem per totum orbem, si vis Christum amare;*
quia membra Christi per orbem iacent"

(*Sanctus Augustinus Hipponensis*)

Contents

Illustrations

MAP

PLATES

Foreword

For those familiar with the iconic imagery of Fatehpur Sikri, Akbar's magnificent but abandoned capital, imagining the intellectual fervor that once animated its courtyards and audience halls is not difficult. This volume by Youri Martini offers a rigorous and compelling exploration of those spaces, both literal and metaphorical, where diverse religious, linguistic, and cultural traditions converged in a complex yet deliberate dialogue. In this context religious diversity became a central axis of political strategy.

This book, organized into five chapters, provides a thorough analysis of the Jesuit missions and their multifaceted interactions with the Mughal court. With rigorous scholarship and its ability to weave together diverse strands of historical inquiry, the author draws on a wealth of primary sources, including Jesuit letters, Mughal chronicles, and Persian texts, to present a detailed account of the Jesuit missions. The opening chapter situates these encounters within the broader framework of Portuguese expansion in India and the global strategies of Jesuit missionary activity. Subsequent chapters critically engage with the theological debates and the roles assumed by the Jesuits at Akbar's court, examining these dynamics through a balanced lens that highlights both their opportunities and limitations.

Particular attention is devoted to the three Jesuit missions, beginning with an analysis of their journey to Fatehpur Sikri and extending to their debates and engagements with Akbar and his court. These discussions explore not only the Jesuits' aims and strategies but also the inherent tensions and negotiations that characterized their presence in a court shaped by complex political, cultural, and religious dynamics.

If the primary focus is on examining the Jesuit missions, the study ultimately provides a comprehensive overview of Akbar's religious policies, providing a framework for understanding the intricate interconnections that defined the Mughal Empire in the sixteenth century.

In a culturally and religiously diverse land, Akbar implemented a policy of inclusivity aimed at consolidating power and maintaining stability. Declaring himself inspired by the Sufi principle of *ṣulḥ-i kull* ("peace with all"), he introduced administrative reforms to reduce religious discrimination and ensure equitable treatment for his subjects. This principle was not limited to "tolerance" but extended to a systematic effort to integrate diverse religious perspectives into a unified imperial framework. Akbar's religious reforms were accompanied by initiatives that facilitated intellectual and cultural exchanges, including the translation of key texts and organized debates among representatives of various religious traditions. Martini meticulously traces how the Jesuits, with their theological rigor and missionary zeal, entered this environment. The Jesuit missions were not only endeavors of religious conversion but also instances of cultural exchange, negotiation, and sometimes tension. The multifaceted role of the Jesuits as diplomats, translators, and cultural mediators is brought to life through Martini's careful analysis, including their use of sacred images, literature, and art as tools for religious instruction, reflects on the impact of Christian art and literature within the Mughal cultural milieu. The author's examination of the theological disputes, the production of Persian Christian literature, and the Mughal fascination with Christian art reveals how the Jesuit missions sought to present Christianity to Akbar through a process of cultural translatability. This approach was rooted in a missionary attempt to render Christian teachings intelligible and appealing within the complex religious and artistic landscape of Mughal India, effectively reinterpreting Christian theology in forms accessible to Akbar and his court.

Martini avoids simplistic narratives of success or failure, instead offering a balanced perspective on the reciprocal influences between the missionaries and their Mughal hosts.

A significant amount of the historiography—initially British and later Indian—produced during the colonial and postcolonial periods had portrayed Akbar as a revolutionary ruler, a pioneer of secularism and tolerance. However, upon closer examination, the concept of tolerance is scarcely applicable to premodern societies, and notions such as secularism or laicism are anachronistic categories that do not align with the context of that era. Akbar himself did not view himself as a secular ruler. Rather than embodying a secularist ideal, Akbar's kingship represents a model rooted in Sufi and millenarian motifs, where sovereignty and sacrality are deeply intertwined. This philosophy, along with an exploration of its religious foundations, is thoroughly examined in the study.

To conclude, this book offers a window into a period of history that remains relatively underexplored in European scholarship, that is an interesting case study of religious openess —or perhaps, better stated, religious accommodation, and also invites readers to consider the potential of intercultural and interreligious exchange as a framework for addressing contemporary challenges.

Elisabetta Colagrossi
(Professor of History of Religions
at the University of Genoa)

Preface to the Italian Edition

On 24 October 2016, Pope Francis, visiting his Jesuit confreres gathered for the election of their new Father General, quoted the words of his predecessor Benedict XVI, 'As my Predecessors have said to you on various occasions, the Church needs you, relies on you and continues to turn to you with trust, particularly to reach those physical and spiritual places which others do not reach or have difficulty in reaching.'[1]

Furthermore, the Pope added that as St Ignatius said, the Jesuit is called 'to travel through the world and to live in any part of it where there is hope of greater service to God and of help of souls'.[2]

Youri Martini's invaluable contribution, which the reader is now fortunate enough to hold in his hands, is an authentically documented attestation of this missionary nature of the members of the Society of Jesus who are ready to 'seek God our Lord in all things'[3] and everywhere. As the first and only Turkish Jesuit from Islam, when asked to write a short Preface, I read this book in an instant and was fascinated not only by the ability of my fellow Jesuits to set out promptly and enculturated themselves with admirable flexibility in 'a reality that is completely different and almost inconceivable to the Western mindset', but also by the figure of Jalal-ud-dìn Muhammad Akbar (1542-1605) whom the author with extraordinary effectiveness and great merit brings to light.

History does not present us with so many other Muslim rulers like Akbar who, even five centuries before our era—and even though he could neither read nor write properly—was very interested in philosophy, fine arts, history and religion. He opened the doors of his palace to the Western clergy to foster dialogue and promote knowledge.

Martini, in fact, while noting Akbar's reformist approach to social and economic affairs—that have undoubtedly brought him to the centre of attention of historians and scholars—enlightens us with great skill on the years in which the ruler reigned in India, years marked not only by religious revival in India but throughout the world. Akbar's religious and political reforms during this period were not only striking for his contemporaries; they place him in an irreplaceable place in the history of relations and dialogue between Islam and Christianity.

Indeed, while massacres were being carried out in the name of religion in various countries of the world, Akbar followed a policy of removing religious discrimination from the Indian society of the time—a multi-religious and multi-cultural policy. As for the conflict between the Muslim, Hindu, Buddhist, Christian and other religions, Akbar's apparent lack of scruples in religious matters prompted him, on the one hand—to adopt a policy inspired by the Sufi principle of *Sulh-i-kul* (universal peace), while on the other hand—to inaugurate the *Din-i Ilahi* which would bring together Islamism, Hinduism, Buddhism, Zoroastrianism and some of the principles of Christianity.

The institution of *Din-i Ilahi*—which was a synthesis that forbade sins such as lust, defamation and pride, and was based on virtues such as equality, freedom, patience, abstinence, support, confidentiality, courtesy among people—was certainly the fruit of Akbar's contacts and long dialogues with religious scholars from different faiths including Catholicism and in particular the Jesuits. Martini helps us to recognize that although Akbar was not successful in his aim—and the *Din-i Ilahi* turned out to be 'a restricted circle of the emperor's intimates, like disciples gathered around a master, similar, in fact, to a Sufic brotherhood'—this open-mindedness of his and the freedom of religion and worship that he had left to his subjects put him in a very prominent place.

Those who read the book will be able to understand that Akbar's intention was not to abjure Islam and adopt a religion of his own invention, as several of his co-religionists accused him of doing. Nor was his real intention to convert to Catholicism as the Jesuits had hoped. In spite of the clear disparity of opinions towards Akbar and the Jesuits, and the complexity of the subject matter, the author must be credited with having been able to offer his own authoritative interpretation, revisiting the developments of this fascinating historical page using a wealth of arguments from a wide range of works by Italian and international scholars.

Martini's work is valuable not only for those interested in the history and inter-religious dialogue between Islam and Christianity, but also because this critical study is a candidate to fill the gap in knowledge of a splendid figure like Akbar who remains one of the few unsurpassed models of religious openness and respect. This work by Martini is also a highly original book that will enrich previous contributions with the history of the Society of Jesus and its fascinating missionary nature.

Antuan Ilgit, S.J.
Auxiliary Bishop of the Apostolic Vicariate of Anatolia (Turkey)
Professor of Moral Theology
Pontifical Theological Faculty of Southern Italy Naples

NOTES

1. Address of Benedict XVI to participants in the General Congregation of the Society of Jesus, 21 February 2008.
2. *The Constitutions of the Society of Jesus*, p. 304.
3. Ibid., p. 288.

Introduction

The figure of Akbar (1542-1605), the third Indian emperor of the Mughal dynasty, is still debated by historians. Many scholars have tried to identify the reasons why a Muslim ruler—to all intents and purposes the sultan of a Sunni theocracy—invited and hosted a group of Catholic missionaries at his court, an almost unique circumstance in history. Among Muslims, Islam is seen as the religion inherent in human beings, while Christianity and Judaism are a deviation from the original faith. So there is no interest in reading the holy books of other religious denominations, an activity that could also be dangerous.

The Mughals did not belong to the Arab ethnic group like other Muslim populations. They were very well aware of the complex and differentiated Indians' socio-religious reality, of the considerable space-time and cultural distance which existed between their world, and that in which their faith was elaborated. Once Akbar had consolidated his power, he began a process of progressive distancing from the dominant Sunnite position in order to adopt a farsighted religious policy which would allow him to win the goodwill of his subjects. For centuries, a Muslim minority in Hindustan had dominated over a Hindu majority population. As will be seen, the emperor, in issuing a series of legislative measures to open up to the various non-Islamic communities, was also influenced by his own religious convictions; These matured following a sincere spiritual search and were influenced more than anything else by the Sufi currents circulating in India at the time. The ruler contemplated a reform of Islam, consisting mainly of an adaptation to Indo-Iranian culture, which could not be achieved without a prior process of relativization of certain essential Muslim dogmas. In this sense, rather than arguments in favour of Christianity, it was the contribution of his anti-Islamic polemic that was useful and interesting. For this reason, the hopes the missionaries had placed in the emperor's conversion were soon dashed. Although the subject is still debated in academic circles, it seems that Akbar intended to attain a power at least comparable to that of the Prophet or the first four Caliphs—a status that would allow him to escape any form of religious control.

The Jesuits in Mughal India came into contact with a completely different reality that was almost inconceivable to the Western mindset. Their activity was characterized by a double orientation—towards the court and towards the local population. Therefore, while some fathers continued their commitment to the pastoral care of the nascent Christian community, others led the life of courtiers, becoming part of the emperor's entourage. As we shall see, the Jesuits themselves developed some missionary strategies on the spot. Mughal India, like other similar places, was a new and equally difficult field of apostolate, for which no adequate preliminary preparation was foreseen at the time. In order to effectively convey the Christian message, the fathers tried to adapt to the cultural reality in which they worked. There were many occasions for the spectacularization of liturgical celebrations, theatrical representations of biblical episodes and the use of sacred images. Contrary to what one might think, European devotional art was welcomed both at the court and by the population. In particular, this mission also provided the occasion for the formation of the first Christian literature in Persian.

As can be seen from the bibliography used, this study has drawn on the contribution of authoritative exponents of the international academic world, whose positions, considering the complexity of the theme in question, are not only different, but sometimes even conflicting. In spite of the difficulties, mainly due to the disparity of opinions, an attempt has been made to offer an interpretation that is as plausible and consistent as possible of the events that constitute the specific subject of this study. To this end, it was obviously necessary and indispensable to make frequent use of contemporary sources relating to our subject. The publications—still in progress—have these precious documentary testimonies. These are often reproduced in a vehicular language such as English, which has made them more accessible to scholars. In this work, in order to facilitate the reading and to avoid a continuous and tedious operation of transposition from one language to another, we have decided to quote sources and studies in the most recent and reliable English translations; where it has not been possible, personal translation has been provided.

MAP: THE INDIA IN THE AGE OF THE EMPIRE OF AKBAR

Source: C. Collin Davies, *An Historical Atlas of the Indian Peninsula*, 2/e, Bombay: Oxforc University Press, 1961.

1 The Jesuits at the Mughal Court

An Atypical Mission

PORTUGUESE AND MISSIONARIES IN INDIA

At the dawn of the sixteenth century, the Indian subcontinent was divided into several dynastic states. To the north was the Sultanate of Delhi, ruled by the Afghan Lodi dynasty and bordered by other Islamic monarchies. A similar situation could also be seen in the south, where the Vijayanagara Empire asserted itself as a hegemonic power over the other Hindu kingdoms.

After the death of Sikandar Lodi (1489-1517), his son Ibrahim (d. 1526) was elected as the new sultan. Unlike his father, Ibrahim was unable to impose his authority and prevent rebellions by the feudal aristocracy, thus favouring the invasion of the army of Babur (reigning from 1483 to 1530), Prince of Kabul. The latter, after the victorious Battle of Panipat in 1526, began the glorious Mughal Empire, which reached its apogee during the reigns of successive emperors. In particular, Akbar managed to consolidate his power with a series of military campaigns aimed at encompassing the surrounding kingdoms, while at the same time aiming to win the consent of large swathes of the population through a policy of reform.[1]

As is well known, India has been a destination for merchants trading in spices, which were essential for food preservation, and precious silk fabrics since ancient times. During the Middle Ages, the maritime republics of Venice and Genoa, through the onerous mediation of the Arabs, played a crucial role in importing these much sought-after exotic products. The Kingdom of Portugal, following Vasco da Gama's landing on the Malabar coast in 1498, quickly established a maritime empire and took over the monopoly of the spice trade.[2]

When Portuguese navigators discovered the route to the East Indies by circumnavigating Africa, the popes had made a number of agreements with the kings of Portugal regarding the evangelization of these lands, given the great interest and zeal of the Lusitanians in promoting the Christian faith.[3] 'The immense territories of southern and eastern Asia and Africa were therefore placed under Portuguese ecclesiastical jurisdiction or *Padroado*.'[4] The king exercised de facto the functions of the pope's vicar, assuming full authority over the mission churches to the point of becoming their patron.

> Accordingly, the Portuguese kings were granted a voice in the appointment of bishops in any sees created in these regions, and in the sending of missionaries; they bound themselves to make the necessary contributions for the maintenance of the missions and their institutions and for the protection of the neophytes.[5]

Portuguese influence in the coastal areas of India contributed greatly to the spread of Christianity, while in the interior of the peninsula, conciliatory and pragmatic rulers such as Akbar and Raja Wadiyar[6] allowed ministers of the Gospel to proselytize and carry out conversions in their territories.[7]

The greatest contribution to evangelization came from the religious orders. In particular, the Jesuits, who started working in India in 1542, soon became not only the most numerous missionary group, but also the one that achieved the best results.[8] The first preachers had not taken into account the complex cultural and religious reality of India, so that the few and often specious conversions were achieved only among members of the lower classes, eager for social redemption. The Jesuits are credited with having understood the need for prior study of indigenous languages and societies to better convey the universal message of Christ.[9] As the *Formula of the Institute* (1540) states, the Jesuits are ready to go wherever there is a need: 'among the Turks or to other infidels, even to the land they call India'.[10] The term 'the Turks' at that time did not designate an ethnic group, but simply the Muslims. From the very beginning, the founder of the Society of Jesus himself, St Ignatius of Loyala (1491-1556),[11] promoted the study of Islamic theology to provide adequate preparation for those who would enter into religious conversation with the 'Mohammedans'.

THE SURPRISING INITIATIVE

The missions undertaken by the Jesuits in northern India, as the French historian Hugues Didier rightly points out, go beyond the usual context of evangelization activities in Asia and, in many respects, also beyond the framework of relations between Christian Europe and the Muslim East. Usually the establishment of a Catholic mission resulted from a decision taken in Rome or Goa or within a religious order. Moreover, the missionaries generally experienced many difficulties in penetrating Asian countries; in fact, only after long and difficult negotiations with the customs officials of the local sovereigns could they obtain special permission to transit or stay in their territories. Now, in the case of Mughal India, it was the Jesuits who were invited by the Muslim ruler Muhammad Abu'l-Fath Jalal-ud-din, better known as Akbar (the Great), thus contradicting the idea that it was always the European or Christian side that took the initiative.[12]

Surprisingly enough, in 1579, the Indian emperor, through his ambassador Haji Habibullah, accompanied by an interpreter, the Armenian Domingo Pires, sent a letter to the Jesuits of the College of St Paul, as well as to the Lusitanian authorities in Goa, in which he requested:

> two learned priests should be sent unto us, to bring the chief books of the Law[13] and the Gospel[14] in order that we may learn the Law and its full meaning and perfect truths in every respect [...]. Let them not hesitate, therefore, to set out with the same envoys [...] and let them bring the books of the Law with them. Let the priests understand that I shall receive them

with all possible kindness and honour. Their arrival will be a great delight to me: and when I have learnt what I long to know about the law and its perfection and the salvation it offers, they shall be allowed to return as soon as they like. I shall send them back again dignified with very many honours and gifts.[15]

Why did Akbar, a Sunni sovereign, ask the Goa authorities for theologians carrying the Holy Scriptures of the Christians? We will try to answer this question by starting from an observation: the Jesuits, as we shall see, immediately participated in the activities of the *Ibadat Khana*, a centre for religious and philosophical studies and a place for inter-confessional theological disputes, and of the *Maktab Khana*, a translation office, which Akbar had established in his capital.[16]

THEOLOGICAL DISPUTES

The Mughal Empire was somewhat atypical, with a religious minority ruling over a majority. Indeed, Akbar, the monarch of a Muslim-Sunnite dynasty (the Mughals), ruled over a predominantly Hindu population. As sultan, however, he had to be first and foremost the temporal ruler of a people who professed the Islamic faith. As a result, he was easily influenced by the *ulama*,[17] mostly Sunni theologians who held a monopoly on the interpretation of the Koran and imposed the application of *Shari'a*, the 'Law of God', as the legal system, exercising strict control over state affairs. Under the pretence of defending public morality and driven by the desire to preserve Islamic doctrine and centuries of tradition, the ulama dared to stand up as champions of orthodoxy not only against Hinduism, but also against other Muslim currents, which they considered heterodox or dissident, or even heretical. They even managed to grab some of the most important public offices, which gave them a privileged position in society.[18] However, their predominant presence in the highest and most powerful positions was no guarantee of peace and harmony: in fact, they were often divided into hostile factions.

The Great Mughal not only realized that it was difficult to achieve cohesion between the Muslim dominants and the Hindu population because of the profound cultural and religious differences, but he also saw a lack of uniformity in the Islamic world itself, which was the result of the different theological interpretations and was the cause of frequent disagreements and conflicts. It seemed impossible to get out of this impasse, but the emperor pressed for a resolution, first by promoting disputes between scholars of different theological positions. To this end in 1575 he had a structure built in his capital Fatehpur Sikri, called *Ibadat Khana* (House of Worship), and announced that every Thursday evening 'who searched after spiritual and physical truth, and those of the common public who sought for an awakening, and the inquiries of every sect should assemble in the precincts of the holy edifice, and bring forward their spiritual experiences'.[19]

Initially, however, only those scholars and Sufis who remained firmly within the doctrinal sphere of Sunni orthodoxy of the Hanafi rite, as well as those who boasted honorary titles such as *sheikh*, *sayyid*, *emir* and *alim*, were invited in the presence of the king and some nobles.[20] It was only later that the doors were also opened to the Shakhites, Shi'ites[21] and other groups who had hitherto been kept on the fringes of official religious life and usually persecuted for their heterodoxy.[22]

Akbar, although he did not know the subtleties of theology, showed a certain ability in posing religious questions, manifesting an evident impatience with the existence within Islam of a variety of interpretations that were often incompatible between themselves. Therefore, in order to settle the theological differences, he requested, through the comparison of the different positions, a critical examination of the Word of God (the Koran) and the words of the Prophet (*Hadith*[23]).[24] The emperor was convinced that man, thanks to the exercise of reason (*aql*) and the use of dialectical argumentation (*jadal*), based on the encounter/clash of opinions, possessed the ability to reach a definitive truth and, therefore, at the opening of an assembly he declared:

> My sole object, oh wise mullahs, is to ascertain the truth, to find out and disclose the principles of genuine religion, and trace it to its divine origin. Take care, therefore, that through the influence of your human passions,

you are not induced to conceal the truth: and say nothing contrary to the almighty decrees. If you do, you are responsible before God for the consequences of your impiety.[25]

To his great disappointment, however, the Great Mughal soon realized the failure of his initiative, because the debates in the *Ibadat Khana* only served to highlight and exacerbate the deep doctrinal differences. Even the chronicler 'Abd al-Qadir Bada'uni (*c.* 1540-1615), an orthodox Sunni, could observe with great indignation how his co-religionists participating in theological disputes were incapable of adopting a single point of view on matters of faith: 'one would pronounce a thing as unlawful, and another by some process of argument would pronounce the very same thing lawful'.[26] This conduct certainly had no correspondence with the doctrine of *ijma*,[27] which excludes the possibility of individual interpretation (*ijtihad*) in favour of unanimous consent.[28]

Moreover, disputes often degenerated into unedifying mutual accusations and clashes, not only verbal but also physical. The *ulama*, as Indian historian Ashirbadi Lal Srivastava writes, 'quarrelled among themselves on fundamental questions of Islamic theology and openly exhibited unworthy intolerance to each other'.[29] Bada'uni bitterly notes that the scholars called 'one another fools and heretics [...] and became very Jews and Egyptians for hatred of each other'.[30] According to the Indian scholar Abraham Eraly, 'the discussions, instead of strengthening Akbar's faith in Islam, in fact shattered it'.[31] Bada'uni reports, indeed, that 'the differences among the ulama [...] became to His Majesty another cause of unbelief'.[32]

THE SOVEREIGN AS MASTER AND GUIDE OF THE FAITHFUL

Faced with the presence in the Islamic world of divergent or antinomian theses that coexisted without arriving at an 'official' dialectical synthesis, towards the end of 1579, the Great Mughal had a measure approved (*mahzar*), the so-called 'Decree of Infallibility',[33] by the main *ulama* of the court, 'some willingly, others against their convictions',[34] to regulate the modalities for the solution of possible theological-moral controversies. The emperor really wanted to put an end to and prevent in the future innumerable and useless discussions caused by the variety and conflict of doctrinal systems. In this document we read, therefore, that the emperor was allowed to 'adopt, for the benefit of the nation and as a political expedient, any of the conflicting opinions' that might exist on a religious question and to 'issue a decree to that effect', with imperative and binding effect for 'the whole nation'.[35] In the *mahzar*, the *ulama* declared that:

> Further, we declare that, should His Majesty think fit to issue a new order, we and the nation shall likewise be bound by it, provided always that such an order be not only in accordance with some verse of the Qur'ān, but also of real benefit for the nation; and further, that any opposition on the part of the subjects to such an order as passed by His Majesty, shall involve damnation in the world to come, and loss of religion and property in this life.[36]

Such a declaration contained nothing against Islam; Indian sultans often possessed immense power, although they exercised limited ability to legislate on religious matters: the *ulama* constantly observed and judged government policy, checking its conformity with the *Shari'a*. However, as Eraly states, 'the stipulations in the declaration, it was evident, could all be easily manipulated by an absolute monarch to make his will prevail'.[37] Indeed, Akbar was able to free himself permanently from the control of the theologians within a short period of time.

A careful reading of the document reveals a not too veiled allusion to the sovereign's desire to free himself definitively from religious power, to free himself from the influence of the Sunni and Shi'ite hierarchies. In fact, the *mahzar* confers on Akbar the title of *imam-i-adil* (just leader), 'the man dearest to God', proclaiming that 'the rank of *sultan-i-adil* [just ruler] is higher in the eyes of God than the rank of a *mujtahid*', the Shi'ite religious authority legitimized to interpret Koranic law. At the same time, the declaration, by also attributing to the emperor the caliphal epithet of *amiru'l muminin* (Commander of the Faithful), placed him above any Sunni religious authority.[38]

The writing of the *mahzar* could therefore also be understood as part of a strategic political purpose with particularly relevant international implications. In fact, as the scholar Milanetti states, who seems to share the opinions of historians such as Buckler[39] and Roy Choudhury,

> the petition of 1579 was nothing more than the instrument with which Akbar affirmed the autonomy and sovereignty of his dynasty with respect to the two powers that then represented the highest expressions of Islamic religious and political authority: the caliphate for the Sunni tradition and the Persian monarchy for the Shi'ite one.[40]

The *mahzar*, by assigning the Great Mughal a higher rank than that of the Iranian *mujtahid*, removed him from the authority of the Shia Shah and, at the same time, by conferring on him the caliphal title of *amiru'l muminin*, intended to proclaim his absolute independence from the authority of the Ottoman Sunni dynasty.[41]

According to Didier, the emperor, in order to curb any possible claims of vassalage made by Safavid Iran and the Sultanate of Istanbul, tried to be recognized as the only master of the Indian Muslims and to become the leader of Islam. It seems that the Great Mughal intended to exploit the hopes of the many popular movements linked to Mahdist millenarianism that were constantly being born and growing in the Indian religious environment.[42]

Mahdism had within it a plurality of currents, different from each other but with fundamental common traits. Firstly, the Mahdists, on the basis of the theory that associated the end of time with the arrival of the year 1000 of the Hegira,[43] awaited the appearance of a *Mahdi* (the well-guided one), a sort of messiah who would renew the whole of creation and bring about the triumph of divine justice. They therefore preached the need for a purification of the whole of society and a return to authentic Islam in view of God's imminent judgement. Thus, in the fifteenth and sixteenth centuries, many spiritual currents were born and spread by charismatic personalities who claimed the title of *Mahdi*, almost overshadowing the figure of the Prophet. These millenarian movements, which in certain aspects revealed some similarities with certain Sufi orders, were characterized by a strong territorial rooting that made them closer to the population and by the fact that they were bearers of an announcement that claimed to address all Muslims. Probably, what could most upset the sensibility of the orthodox Sunnites was the presumed arrogance of not recognizing in the consensus of the *ulama* a form of authorship in Islam.[44]

Akbar, who intended, more than anything else, to keep these movements under control, so that they would not develop in an anarchic manner and, above all, would not provoke a series of agitations, aspired to appear, in the eyes of the followers of millenarianism, as the bearer of messianic hopes, He was therefore particularly suited to be compared to the eschatological figure of the *Mahdi*, as well as perfectly embodying the model of the *Insan al-kamil* (Perfect Man or Universal Man)[45] of the esoteric speculations of Islam, as the source of spiritual and material well-being of its subjects.[46]

Exploiting and at the same time reinforcing the climate of enthusiasm that animated confused millenarian hopes of a renewed world, the emperor, without taking any time in between, took the surprising initiative of reforming the calendar: 'The Hegira era was abolished, and a new era beginning with Akbar's accession, called *Tarikh-i-Ilahi*, was introduced.'[47] The Great Mughal assumed a new epithet, *Khalkifa al-Zaman* (Caliph of Time), which recalled close links with Mahdist chiliasm and indicated the ruler as the supreme guide of the new millennium.[48]

THE TRANSLATION OFFICE

At the same time as his theological debates, the Great Mughal cultivated an intense passion for manuscripts, which he regarded as works of art in preference to printed books, and was enchanted by the virtuosities of calligraphy and magnificent illustrations.[49] Since not a few scholars are inclined to admit Akbar's illiteracy,[50] one might assume that his interest in manuscripts was purely aesthetic. Nevertheless, he was a monarch who was highly appreciated for his sensitivity to literary works and already during his lifetime enjoyed a wide reputation as a sage.[51] According to the chronicler of the Jesuits' first mission to the Mughal court, Anthony Monserrate (1536-1600), Akbar was not only surprisingly well informed about all the affairs of the empire, but also possessed a culture and knew about philosophy and art; listening to him, no one would ever have suspected him of being unable to read and write.[52]

In any case, as Eraly rightly points out, 'Being unlettered was not, however, a disability in the Mughal emperor—there was no functional need for him to be literate, for he could always hire people to read and write for him.'[53]

Around the emperor, flourished a court attended by the most eminent scholars of the time and of different cultural, religious and linguistic backgrounds. Immersed in such a stimulating intellectual environment, the Great Mughal was keen to have at his disposal, in an accessible language, namely Persian, now the language of the court, the military elite, the nobility, the government and the public administration, a great variety of classical works in almost all branches of human knowledge then known. Therefore, he had his own translation office, the *Maktab Khana*, established in 1575 with the aim of founding a massive library in the Persian language,[54] including all the sacred books of mankind and other works such as classics of philosophy and science originally composed in Arabic, Sanskrit, Greek, Latin and other European languages.[55] Within this office, a well-organized scriptorium was set up that employed specialists from various fields such as *pandits*,[56] calligraphers and proof-readers.[57]

As a first initiative of the *Maktab Khana*, it was decided to translate the texts related to the different faiths that contributed to the spiritual variety of India. This variety consisted of a collection of religious communities that seemed to be isolated monads imprisoned within themselves, with no sign of opening up to the outside world. If we consider, therefore, the lack of a common language comprehensible to all subjects, the already difficult realization of a peaceful coexistence of the religious groups, as well as the mutual disinterest in their relations, any possibility of interchange that went beyond mere questions of political expediency seemed precluded. For Muslims, the Koran is the material realization of the eternal Truth found with God, so reading or knowing the texts of other religions is almost useless, if not harmful. The Hindus and other Indian religious groups, on their part, as jealous guardians of their millenary spiritual traditions, were disinclined to have wide access to the contents of their sacred books.

Did Akbar through the activities of the *Maktab Khana* really intend to help overcome cultural and religious barriers? Did he aim at promoting proper mutual understanding between different ethnic groups? It is difficult to understand what the Great Mughal had in mind. Hypothetically, one could, however, include the *Maktab Khana* in a wider and more ambitious project that envisaged the progressive Iranization of Indian culture and customs, up to the official recognition of Persian as a pan-Indian language. The many contacts and diplomatic relations since his childhood with the Safavid court, the presence at the palace of a group of nobles and scholars from Persia and, above all, the consequent opportunity to rediscover the classics of Iranian mysticism, meant that the sovereign became accustomed to the use of Persian. He preferred it to Turkish, the language of his lineage; to Arabic, the language of Koranic revelation, studied, known and spoken by the majority of Muslims; and to all the vernacular languages of India, thus avoiding the political difficulties that the choice of a local language as a lingua franca would have entailed. Akbar was well aware that this preference could arouse the disdain of conservative Sunni circles, but he was willing to run this risk, because he was aware that Persian, as a member of the Indo-European family of languages, like most Indian languages, was more accessible and comprehensible to the people and reasonably easier to learn and speak than Arabic, of Semitic origin.[58]

Important works belonging to the Hindu tradition were translated, such as the *Mahabharata*,[59] the *Atharva Veda*[60] and the *Ramayana*.[61] As for the Koran, some Persian versions[62] were already circulating, although the Islamic tradition has always been against the translation of the holy book into other languages.[63]

THE ROLE OF THE JESUITS

The activity of the *Maktab Khana* soon proved to be fundamental in order to gain access to India's spiritual, religious and philosophical tradition, although objectively varied and complex. The reading of the classics of Hinduism, a faith professed by the vast majority of its population, could only stimulate even more interest in the emperor with his increasingly eclectic curiosity in the vast body of religious thought formed in India. Therefore, Akbar soon declared his intention to open the doors of the *Ibadat Khana* to 'learned men of all religions, thus deriving profit from their exquisite discourses and exalted aspirations'.[64] The emperor was no longer willing to limit the theological debate solely to different interpretations and representations of Islam. The disputing scholars, moreover, had exacerbated the divergences with their constant violent quarrels.[65] As a consequence, the sovereign did his utmost to ensure an ever-wider participation of representatives of the various faiths that make up the variegated Indian religious panorama. From 1578 onwards, Hindus, Sikhs, Parsis,[66] Buddhists, Jews, Christians, Jains, Sabians[67] and Charvakas[68] were invited to theological debates. The Great Mughal explained that it was his intention to bring together people of different faiths for a peaceful discussion of their differences.[69]

The arrival of the Jesuits could also offer an effective collaboration within the *Maktab Khana*. Already in 1578 the Great Mughal had commissioned his most faithful advisor, Abu'l-Fadl, to translate the Gospel, an initiative that greatly disconcerted the orthodox Sunni circles.[70] A few centuries before the Mughal period, Persian-speaking Jews and Christians, probably Nestorians, living in Iran, had translated the Bible from Hebrew, Aramaic or Syriac.[71] As one might deduce from the account of the Portuguese chronicler Diogo do Couto (1542-1616), although there is not enough data to support this hypothesis, Emperor Humayun (1508-56), Akbar's father, may have had a Persian version of the Holy Scripture at his disposal during his exile to Shah Tahmasp I (1514-76).[72] However, for the period of Akbar's reign, we have no information about direct research at the Safavid court by Mughal emissaries. Presumably in the years 1578-9, the ruler, before resorting to the Jesuits, had sent his diplomatic official Sayyd Muzaffar to the Middle East with the task of finding Arabic or Persian translations of the Pentateuch, Psalms and Gospels,[73] but he proved unable to convince the Christian communities of Mesopotamia, Syria or Egypt to surrender their precious manuscripts.[74]

AKBAR AND THE PORTUGUESE

The sovereign's initiative to invite some Jesuit fathers to his court, although inspired, as we shall see, also by religious motivations, was part of the fluctuating diplomatic and commercial relations between the Mughal and Lusitanian governments.

In the first fifteen years of his reign, Akbar had managed to conquer a large part of northern India thanks to the success of his aggressive expansionist policy, but he was not satisfied with his predominantly mountainous and landlocked territory, so he turned his attention to Gujarat, a region overlooking the Arabian Sea. He also wanted to conquer this sultanate in order to halt the gradual advance of the Portuguese, who now held a maritime empire stretching from West Africa to the Far East, made up almost exclusively of coastal cities. In 1510 they had definitively settled in the Indian Peninsula, having conquered Goa,[75] a locality of considerable importance, which, given its strategic position controlling important maritime communication routes, soon became the centre of colonial power as well as the capital of a viceroyalty dependent on the Court of Lisbon. Within a short time, the Lusitanian colonists founded a series of fortified settlements along the Indian coast and occupied other important port cities such as Daman[76] and Diu,[77] but, clearly not yet satisfied with their power, they intended to further extend their dominion along the north-west coast.

These Europeans already had a monopoly on the sea routes and imposed taxes on all merchant ships crossing the Indian seas, even those carrying Muslim worshippers to or from Mecca, as the transport of pilgrims was considered a commercial traffic in its own right. For the Indians who travelled by land, their Sunni religion made them subject to harassment by the Shi'ite government in Persia, and there was little that the Mamluks and Ottomans could do to protect the caravans of these pilgrims from the raids of the Bedouins.[78] All that remained was the sea route, for which the emperor rented a fleet of a hundred ships; but the crossing required good relations with those who controlled it. Pilgrims were in fact forced to buy Portuguese passports (*cartaz*), bearing images of the Cross and Mary, thanks to which the Portuguese were able to further increase their profits. Not only that, but Lusitanian soldiers and sailors often committed acts of piracy against these pious travellers, so that a large part of the Sunni faithful lobbied hard for the emperor to intervene to put an end to these attacks and ensure the safety of the pilgrims.[79] Nevertheless, the sovereign was particularly interested in controlling maritime traffic: Gujarat, because of its strategic geographical location, was a potential centre of trade between India, Turkey, Syria, Persia, Transoxiana and European countries. The conquest of the sultanate would also have allowed the Mughal Empire to form not only a merchant but also a military navy, and thus challenge the Lusitanian maritime power.

Since the death of Sultan Bahadur Shah (1537) Gujarat had been torn apart by continuous infighting between the nobles who were vying for the crown. In July 1572 Akbar received an urgent appeal from the ambitious tutor of the young Sultan Muzaffar Shah III, Itimad Khan, asking him to intervene on his behalf, promising loyalty and vassalage to the Mughal Empire.[80] The occupation of Gujarat did not meet with much resistance: Akbar conquered important commercial cities such as Ahmedabad[81] and Khambhat[82] and easily subdued the contenders to the throne of the sultanate. In Khambhat he also received the homage of some Indian and Portuguese merchants, who were particularly impressed by the Western-style clothing, so he wanted to buy European clothes and accessories.[83]

Akbar allowed Itimad Khan to retain command of his army as an ally of the Mughals,[84] while forcing Muzaffar Shah III to retire from the political scene and support himself with a pension paid from the imperial treasury.[85] But soon both Muzaffar Shah and Itimad Khan were promoting the cause of independence and were therefore arrested and imprisoned as traitors. The Great Mughal consequently appointed his milk brother, Aziz Koka (1542-1624), as governor of Gujarat.[86]

The emperor had no difficulty in continuing his military campaign, scoring numerous successes and conquering important urban centres such as Vadodara,[87] Champaner[88] and Surat.[89] During the siege of the latter city, Akbar became aware of the presence of some Portuguese, who came to the defence of the besieged, but, seeing the mighty Mughal army, decided not to intervene militarily and not to take sides in the conflict.[90] In the meantime, the viceroy António de Noronha, fearing an imminent attack on the Lusitanian fortresses closest to Gujarat, had quickly reached Daman, where he received with great cordiality an imperial envoy, who had probably come to know the real intentions of the Portuguese and to guarantee their neutrality. The Mughal official then accompanied a captain, Antonio Cabral, who had been sent by the Viceroy on a diplomatic mission to the Great Mughal, who was at the time encamped at the gates of Surat to organize his army.[91] The embassy was received with all honours and the emperor appreciated the exotic and charming gifts that the captain brought with him, directing many questions to him about Europe and the Christian religion,[92] and was again fascinated by the European-style clothing.[93] The two parties reached an agreement: the Mughals obtained permission to transit in the waters controlled by the Lusitanian navy for ships loaded with merchandise or carrying pilgrims without the payment of any customs duty and protected from possible looting, while the Portuguese received in exchange the recognition of their possessions along the Indian coast. After the capitulation of Surat and having secured his dominion over the region, on 18 March 1573 Akbar had a petanum drawn up to be sent to all the officials of the empire, especially those in Gujarat, in which he warned them to refrain from invading the Portuguese colonies and not to favour the Malabar pirates, who were responsible for raids on the Portuguese maritime trade.[94]

Once the victorious Gujarat campaign was over, on 3 June 1573, the emperor made the return journey to Sikri, which soon became the new capital, renaming it Fatehpur (City of Victory), from where he turned his attention to Bengal, intending to obtain an outlet to the east as well. After yet another military triumph, the sovereign resumed diplomatic relations with the Portuguese, sending a mission in 1575 to the new viceroy of Goa, Antonio Moniz Barreto, led by Haji Habibullah, who presented the Portuguese governor with a gift of two fine brocade robes and a velvet cap with gold decoration in the Portuguese style produced by the imperial tailor's atelier. The agreements made at Surat were confirmed: the Portuguese were officially guaranteed not to be attacked by the Mughal militia, while Akbar was able to organize an annual pilgrimage for his Muslim subjects by sea without the payment of taxes and tolls.[95] In 1576, a ministry (*mir i-hajj*) was specifically set up in Mughal India, whereby each pilgrim could receive a viaticum of Rs. 600 from the state.[96]

Other reasons prompted the Great Mughal to send an embassy

to Goa in 1575. Haji Habibullah had brought with him a large sum of money to buy artistic and cultural goods and clothing typical of European countries. He also gathered a retinue of skilled craftsmen to learn and develop new techniques. Staying for three years in the Portuguese capital, Haji Habibullah and his companions returned to their country dressed in Western attire, underlining their return to the city of Fatehpur Sikri with repeated drum rolls and blaring of European trumpets, and soon demonstrated their acquired craftsmanship skills. They delivered to Akbar numerous exotic and precious products, among which a pipe organ, decorated with sacred images representing Jesus and some saints: to enchant the Great Mughal with the sounds of this instrument, it seems that a skilled organist was brought to the court.[97]

AKBAR AND CHRISTIANITY

As we have seen, the Mughal government, in parallel with its military campaigns, concentrated its diplomatic activity on establishing good neighbourly relations with the Portuguese power.

From the various Portuguese posts, some of the most enterprising travellers and merchants, but also discharged soldiers or deserters as well as individuals wanted by the law, had gone far beyond the area of Lusitanian influence, settling in particular along the low and sandy coast of the Bay of Bengal. Released from the control of the mother country and thanks to the good relations established with the local population and rulers, they founded a series of fortified settlements in and around the Ganges Delta. When Akbar took possession of Bengal in 1575, after a military campaign that lasted almost three years, these Europeans had developed a flourishing trade, giving rise to mercantile and trading activities, and many of them had decided to sell their swords as mercenaries in the service of various armies.[98]

In 1576, at the request of the Bishop of Kochi,[99] Henrique de Tavora e Brito,[100] two Jesuit fathers, Antonio Vaz and Pedro Diaz, were sent on a temporary mission to Bengal, with the task of providing spiritual assistance to the many Portuguese who were now permanent residents in the region.[101] The two religious disapproved of the behaviour of many of their fellow countrymen who refused to pay tribute to the Great Mughal and considered that there was a just reason to defer their absolution. The episode also had an echo at the imperial court: the sovereign could only applaud the fathers' initiative and was driven by a desire to learn more about a religion that insisted so much on the need for honest conduct.[102]

In 1577 the Portuguese Pedro Tavares, defined by Akbar's main biographer, Abu'l-Fadl, as 'one of the chief merchants of the ports of Bengal', 'was graciously received at [the] Court, and his sound sense and upright conduct won the favour and esteem of the Emperor',[103] from whom he obtained important concessions for his countrymen. During his stay in Fatehpur Sikri he also had the opportunity to speak to the sovereign about Christianity,[104] who may have expressed to him his wish to have an expert at his court who could participate as a representative of the Catholic Church in the theological disputes generally held in the *Ibadat Khana*. Tavares pointed out to him a certain Gil Eneas Pereira, a diocesan priest, presumably of Indian origin, who was currently residing in Saptagram,[105] where he had been sent by Bishop Henrique de Tavora e Brito as vicar general of Bengal, to provide for the Portuguese living in that region.[106] On 8 March 1578 Pereira arrived in Fatehpur Sikri, where he received a friendly welcome and remained a guest in the imperial palace, with the specific task of privately instructing the sovereign. Soon he started to take part in theological debates, but, being more a man of piety than a fine theologian, he was unprepared to stand comparison with experienced Muslim theologians. So, he advised the sovereign to ask the Goa authorities for some Jesuits from St Paul's College. Thus, it was that the Great Mughal sent again in 1579 his emissary Haji Habibullah to the capital of the *Estado da Índia*, with the task of accompanying to Fatehpur Sikri the theological fathers chosen for the mission.[107]

NOTES

1. This is not the place to outline, even in broad strokes, the history of Mughal India. For an initial in-depth study of the subject, the following texts can be consulted: A. Eraly, *The Mughal Throne: The Saga of India's Great Emperors* (London: W&N, 2004); and J.F Richards, *The Mughal Empire* (Cambridge: Cambridge University Press, 1993).

2. For an extensive discussion of the history of the Portuguese colonial empire, see S. Subrahmanyam, *The Portuguese Empire in Asia. 1500-1700* (Hoboken: Wiley-Blackwell, 2012).
3. J. Thekkedath, *History of Christianity in India*, II (Bangalore: Church History Association of India, 2001), p. 5.
4. Ibid.
5. Ibid. On the Portuguese Patronage, see A. da Silva Rego, *Le Patronage portugais de l'Orient* (Lisbon: Agencia Geral do Ultramar, 1957).
6. Sovereign of the Kingdom of Mysore from 1578 to 1617.
7. Thekkedath, *History of Christianity in India*, p. 3.
8. Ibid., pp. 6-7.
9. On the presence of Jesuits in India, see J. Correia-Afonso, *The Jesuits in India, 1542-1773* (Anand: Gujarat Sahitya Prakash, 1997).
10. *Formula Instituti Societatis Jesu*, n. 3.
11. For a more in-depth look at the life and works of St Ignatius of Loyola, see the following work: A. Ravier, *Ignatius of Loyola and the Founding of the Society of Jesus* (San Francisco: Ignatius Press, 1987).
12. H. Didier, 'Muslim Heterodoxy, Persian Murtaddun and Jesuit Missionaries at the Court of King Akbar (1580-1605)', *The Heythrop Journal*, vol. 49, no. 6 (2008), pp. 898-939; and id., 'Les jésuites auprès du Grand Mogol Akbar (fin xvie siècle): une mission chrétienne atypique auprès d'un souvrain musulman atypique?', in B. Heyberger and R. Madinier (eds), *L'Islam des marges: mission chrétienne et espaces périphériques du monde musulman XVI-XXe siècles* (Paris: Karthala, 2011), p. 17; id., 'Ormuz, point d'appui de la mission des Jésuites auprès du Roy Akbar (années 1580-1605)', in D. Couto and R.M. Loureiro (eds), *Revisiting Hormuz: Portuguese Interactions in the Persian Gulf Region in the Early Modern Period* (Wiesbaden: Otto Harrassowitz GmbH & Co.KG, 2008), p. 163.
13. The Old Testament.
14. The New Testament.
15. Firman of Emperor Akbar to the Jesuits of St Paul's College, Goa, December 1578, in J.S. Hoyland and S.N. Banerjee (eds), *The Commentary of Father Monserrate: S.J., on His Journey to the Court of Akbar* (Oxford: Oxford University Press, 1922). 'Firman' is a word derived from the Persian *farman*, meaning decree, order. It is a royal decree issued by a ruler in some Muslim states such as the Ottoman Empire, the Mughal Empire and the princely state of Hyderabad. In our specific case, however, the term is used to refer to a letter of a diplomatic nature.

16. H. Didier, 'Muslim Heterodoxy', p. 900; and id., 'Les jésuites auprès du Grand Mogol Akbar', pp. 19-20; id., 'Jérome Xavier, conseiller chrétien d'Akbar (1542-1605), roi aussi machiavélique que musulman?', in M.T. Urvoy (ed.), *Islam et christianisme. Éthique et politique* (Paris: Éditions de Paris, 2010), p. 105.
17. Plural of *alim*, theologian, usually Sunni, of Islam. The term *mullah*, which usually designates a Persian-speaking Muslim scholar of the Shia faith, is sometimes used as a synonym for *alim*.
18. K. Lê Thành, *Islam. La storia, le istituzioni, le differenze culturali* (Rome: Armando Editore, 2001), p. 128.
19. Abu'l Fazl, *Akbarnama*, vol. III (Delhi: Low Price Publications, 2007), p. 158.
20. M.L. Roy Choudhury, *The Din-i-Ilahi or the Religion of Akbar* (New Delhi: Munshiram Manoharlal, 1952), pp. 43-5.
21. The emperor had established closer relations with representatives of Shi'ism, such as Mullah Muhammad of Yazdi, with whom he used to hold private talks at night.
22. Bada'uni, *Muntakhab al-Tawarikh*, vol. II (New Delhi: Saeed International, 1990), p. 262.
23. *Hadith* is used as both a singular and a collective plural in English. Sayings, speeches, stories, and acts attributed to Muhammad or his companions.
24. Bada'uni, *Muntakhab al-Tawarikh*, p. 203; and M.L. Roy Choudhury, *The Din-i-Ilahi or the Religion of Akbar*, p. 45.
25. Nuru'l haq, *Zubdatu't Tawarikh*, quoted in S.A.A. Rizvi, 'Dimensions of Sulh-i Kul (Universal Peace) in Akbar's Reign and the Sufi Theory of Perfect Man', in I.A. Khan (ed.), *Akbar and His Age* (Delhi: Northern Book Centre, 1999), p. 8.
26. Bada'uni, *Muntakhab al-Tawarikh*, quoted in A. Eraly, *Emperors of the Peacock Throne: The Saga of the Great Mughals* (London, Penguin Books, 2001), p. 189.
27. The *ijma* (consensus of the doctors of the Law) is the third source of law, after the Koran and the Sunna and before the *qiyas* (analogical reasoning) and the *ray* (personal opinion).
28. G.G. Nastri, *Libertà della fede. Necessità della ragione. Costruzione della filosofia al di là dell'influenza cartesiana protestante* (Rome: Armando Editore, 2009), p. 385.
29. A.L. Srivastava, *A Short History of Akbar the Great (1542-1605)* (Agra: Shiva Lal Agarwala, 1957), p. 53.
30. Bada'uni, *Muntakhab al-Tawarikh*, II, p. 262.

31. A. Eraly, *Emperors of the Peacock Throne*, p. 189.
32. Bada'uni, *Muntakhab al-Tawarikh*, II, p. 262.
33. As defined perhaps improperly by the author of one of the most important biographies on Akbar, the Irish historian and Indianist Vincent Arthur Smith (*Akbar the Great Mogul* [Delhi: S. Chand & Co., 1962]).
34. Bada'uni, *Muntakhab al-Tawarikh*, II, p. 278.
35. Abu'l-Fadl, *Ain-i-Akbari*, vol. I, p. 186.
36. Ibid., p. 204.
37. Ibid., pp. 204-5.
38. G. Milanetti, 'Religione e religioni alla corte di Akbar', in G.C. Calza (ed.), *Akbar. Il grande imperatore dell'India* (Rome: Skira, 2012), p. 55.
39. F.W. Buckler, 'A New Interpretation of Akbar's Infallibility Decree of 1579', *Journal of the Royal Asiatic Society*, vol. 10 (1924).
40. G. Milanetti, 'Religione e religioni alla corte di Akbar', p. 55.
41. Ibid.
42. H. Didier, *Fantomes d'Islam et de Chine. Le voyage de Bento de Gois s.j. (1603-1607)* (Paris: Chandeigne, 2003), pp. 228-9.
43. The year 1000 of the Hegira corresponds to 1591 of the Gregorian date.
44. D. Matringe, *Un Islam non arabe. Horizons indiens et pakistanais* (Paris: Téraèdre, 2005), p. 128.
45. A term designating the man who has successfully achieved his spiritual realization, i.e. unification with the fullness of Godhead.
46. H. Didier, *Fantomes d'Islam et de Chine*, pp. 228-30.
47. A. Eraly, *Emperors of the Peacock Throne*, p. 200.
48. H. Didier, *Fantomes d'Islam et de Chine*, p. 229.
49. A. Eraly, *Emperors of the Peacock Throne*, p. 174.
50. The question of Akbar's illiteracy has triggered an ongoing debate. According to Indian historian M. Athar Ali, Akbar's illiteracy was mainly an artifice by Abu'l-Fadl (1551-1602), the ruler's secretary and official biographer, to establish the 'divinity' of his knowledge and wisdom and thus compare him to Muhammad, the *an-nabi-'l-ummi* ('the illiterate prophet') (M. Athar Ali, *Mughal India: Studies in Polity, Ideas, Society, and Culture* [New Delhi: Oxford University Press, 2006], p. 159). In fact, the imperial chronicler states that it was clear that 'the lofty comprehension of this Lord of the Age was not learned or acquired, but was the gift of God in which human effort had no part' (Abu'l-Fadl, *Ain-i-Akbari*, vol. I, p. 589). Recent studies support the

view that his difficulty in reading and writing was due to dyslexia problems (G.C. Calza, 'Akbar. Il più grande', in id. [ed.], *Akbar*, p. 14).

51. A. Eraly, *Emperors of the Peacock Throne*, p. 174.
52. J.S. Hoyland and S.N. Banerjee (eds), *The Commentary of Father Monserrate, S.J.*, p. 201. English scholar and colonel Thomas Wolseley Haig (1865-1938) argued that, 'In spite of his illiteracy he was far from being unlearned, nor was his intellect uncultivated, for he delighted in listening to the reading of works of history, theology, philosophy and other subjects, and of discussing afterwards what had been read' (W. Haig, *The Cambridge History of India*, vol. IV: *The Mughul Period* [Cambridge University Press, 1937], p. 154). Similarly, his heir Salim, future emperor Jahangir (1569-1627), had written: 'although he was illiterate, so much became clear to him through constant intercourse with the learned and wise, in his conversations with them, that no one knew him to be illiterate, and he was so acquainted with the niceties of prose and verse composition that this deficiency was not thought of' (Jahangir, *Tūzuk-i-Jahāngīrī*, quoted in S.M. Burke, *Akbar: The Greatest Mogul* [New Delhi: Munshiram Manoharlal, 1989], p. 92).
53. A. Eraly, *Emperors of the Peacock Throne*, p. 174. Similarly, the Austrian scholar Hans-Georg Behr (1937-2010) states that 'in the life of medieval princes, this question was of little importance: writing was the task of the secretaries, there was no order that was not dictated; in the final analysis it proved advantageous to listen to the information out loud; Akbar thus learned to form an opinion by continually discussing the arguments verbally' (H. Behr, *I moghul. Imperatori dell'India* [Milan: Garzanti, 1985], p. 112). Abu'l-Fadl notes that, 'Experienced people bring them [literary works] daily and read them before His Majesty, who hears every book from the beginning to the end. At whatever page the readers daily stop, His Majesty makes with his own pen a sign, according to the number of the pages; and rewards the readers with presents of cash, either in gold or silver, according to the number of leaves read out by them' (Abu'l-Fadl, *Ain-i Akbari*, I, p. 103).
54. Eraly states that Akbar 'possessed a vast personal library, which, according to an inventory said to have been taken of his treasures after his death, contained 24,000 volumes, valued at 6.5 million rupees' (A. Eraly, *Emperors of the Peacock Throne*, p. 174).
55. H. Didier, 'Les jésuites auprès du Grand Mogol Akbar', p. 20.
56. Honorary title granted in India to scholars particularly skilled in Sanskrit, religion, music and philosophy.

57. S.A.A. Rizvi and V.J. Adams Flynn, *Fatehpur Sikri* (Mumbai: D.B. Taraporevala Sons, 1975), p. 42.
58. H. Didier, *Fantomes d'Islam et de Chine*, pp. 223-4.
59. Written in Sanskrit, it is regarded as the greatest poem of Hindu mythology. Bada'uni with concealed resentment had to collaborate on the translation of the Mahabharata, while Abu'l-Fadl contributed a long Preface.
60. Sacred text of Hinduism recognized as the fourth Veda.
61. Like the *Mahabharata*, it is a mythological poem.
62. The first complete translation of the Koran into Persian dates back to the tenth century.
63. According to the dogma of the untranslatability of the Koran, the Arabic language itself is in the Koran the form of divine manifestation: 'the Word of God is by its nature bound to the language in which it was revealed. The Qur'an itself insists on its Arabic character' (M. Cuypers and G. Gobillot, *Le Coran* [Paris: Le Cavalier Bleu, 2007], p. 36): 'It is a Book whose verses are perfectly explained—a Qur'an in Arabic for people who know' (Surah 41: 3). 'For the Muslim tradition, the letter and the content are inseparable, and both are integral parts of Revelation [...]. To the sacred character of the letter of the Arabic text is added the idea of the inimitability (*i'jaz*) of the Koran' both in meaning and form: being, therefore, 'inimitable, the Qur'an is *a fortiori* untranslatable' (ibid., p. 37).
64. A letter from Akbar to Philip II dated 1582, quoted in A. Eraly, *Emperors of the Peacock Throne*, p. 192.
65. With particular reference to these learned disputants Srivastava writes: 'Their irresponsible behavior and quarrels, their inability to explain satisfactorily the fundamental doctrines of Islam and their personal greed and unworthy conduct convinced Akbar that the truth must be sought' (Srivastava, *A Short History of Akbar the Great*, p. 53).
66. They are the followers of Parsism, a confession derived from Zoroastrianism. During the conquest and Islamization of Persia by the Muslim Arabs, part of the Persian population settled in India.
67. An obscure Semitic sect.
68. According to the Indian scholar Amartya Sen, this was an atheist school, which denied both the existence of God and the soul (A. Sen, *The Argumentative Indian: Writings on Indian History* [London: Penguin, 2006], p. 24).
69. L. Frédéric, *Akbar le Grand Moghol* (Paris: Denoel, 1986), p. 236.
70. H. Didier, 'Muslim Heterodoxy', p. 901; id., *Fantomes d'Islam et de*

Chine, p. 217; and id., 'Les jésuites auprès du Grand Mogol Akbar', p. 20.

71. Id., *Fantomes d'Islam et de Chine*, p. 217.
72. It seems that Emperor Humayun had also shown some interest in the Christian religion, as one can deduce from an anecdote in Diogo do Couto's *Décadas da Asia* about a Portuguese named Cosmo Correa who had taken refuge at the Mughal court. It is said that Humayun, leafing through a richly illuminated Book of Hours—which Cosmo Correa had with him—and after noticing at the beginning of the seven penitential psalms a miniature depicting David and Bathsheba, told his Portuguese host that he knew the relevant biblical passage and wanted to expose it immediately to prove the truth of his statement (D. do Couto, *Da Asia*, Década Quinta, Parte segunda [Lisbon: Regia Officina Typografica, 1780], pp. 260-1). The episode of David's sin with Bathsheba is not mentioned in the Koran, in which the prophets are never depicted as prey to human passions. Therefore, if the account of Diogo do Couto is to be believed, it would perhaps not be entirely unreasonable to assume that the emperor came into possession of a Persian version of the Bible during his exile at the Safavid court.
73. K.A. Nizami, *Akbar and Religion* (Delhi: Idarah-i-Adabiyat-i-Delli, 1989), p. 202.
74. H. Didier, 'Muslim Heterodoxy', p. 900.
75. Currently, it is the smallest state in India in terms of area.
76. Currently, it is the capital of the Daman district in the federated territory of Daman and Diu.
77. Currently, it is the capital of the Diu district in the federated territory of Daman and Diu.
78. A. Baldussi, 'Dalla periferia al centro', in A. Baldussi, P. Manduchi and N. Melis (eds), *Le mille e una strada. Viaggiare pellegrini nel mondo musulmano* (Milan: Franco Angeli, 2005), p. 160.
79. L. Frédéric, *Akbar le Grand Moghol*, pp. 175-6; and K.S. Mathew, 'Akbar and the Europeans: A Study of Changing Perspectives', in I.A. Khan (ed.), *Akbar and His Age*, pp. 114-15.
80. L. Frédéric, *Akbar le Grand Moghol*, pp. 174, 176; and J.L. Metha, *Advanced Study in the History of Medieval India*, vol. II (New Delhi: Sterling Publishers, 1986), pp. 246-7.
81. Currently, it is the capital of Ahmedabad district in the federal state of Gujarat.
82. Currently, it is a town in Anand district of the federal state of Gujarat.
83. N. Vassallo e Silva, 'Precious Stones, Jewels and Cameos: Jacques

de Coutre's Journey to Goa and Agra', in J. Flores and N. Vassallo e Silva (eds), *Goa and the Great Mughal* (Lisbon: Calouste Gulbenkian Foundation, 2004), p. 118.

84. J.L. Metha, *Advanced Study in the History of Medieval India*, p. 247.
85. A. Eraly, *Emperors of the Peacock Throne*, p. 147.
86. J.L. Metha, *Advanced Study in the History of Medieval India*, p. 247.
87. Currently, it is the capital of Vadodara district in the federal state of Gujarat.
88. A city in the federated state of Gujarat.
89. Currently, it is the capital of Surat district in the federal state of Gujarat.
90. L. Frédéric, *Akbar le Grand Moghol*, p. 183.
91. J. Flores and A. Vasconcelos de Saldanha, *Os Firangis na chancelaria mogol. Cópias Portuguesas de documentos de Akbar (1572-1604)* (New Delhi: Embaixada de Portugal, 2003), p. 21.
92. L. Frédéric, *Akbar le Grand Moghol*, p. 183.
93. N. Vassallo e Silva, 'Precious Stones, Jewels and Cameos', p. 118.
94. K.S. Mathew, *Portuguese and the Sultanate of Gujarat* (Delhi: Mittal Publications, 1986), pp. 142-3, 240-1; and id., 'Akbar and the Europeans', p. 116.
95. N. Vassallo e Silva, 'Precious Stones, Jewels and Cameos', pp. 116-18.
96. H. Didier, *Fantomes d'Islam et de Chine*, pp. 215-16.
97. S. Stronge, 'Il Libro di Akbar (Akbarnama) e la cultura di corte in epoca moghul', in G.C. Calza (ed.), *Akbar*, pp. 23-4.
98. J.C. Boyajian, *Portuguese Trade in Asia Under the Habsburgs, 1580-1640* (Baltimore: Johns Hopkins University Press, 2007), pp. 32-3; M. Newitt, *A History of Portuguese Overseas Expansion 1400-1668* (London: Routledge, 2004), pp. 134-5; and P. Malekandathil, *Trade, Religion and Polity in the Indian Ocean* (Delhi: Primus Books, 2010), pp. 70-2.
99. Currently, it is a city located in the Indian federal state of Kerala.
100. He was the Bishop of Kochi until 1577, then Archbishop of Goa until his death in 1581.
101. K.S. Mathew, 'Akbar and the Europeans', pp. 117, 127.
102. P. du Jarric, *Histoire des choses plus mémorables advenues tant* és *Indes Orientale qu'autres pays de la descouverte des Portugais en l'establissement et progrez de la foy Chrestienne et Catholique*, vol. I (Bordeaux: S. Millanges, 1610), p. 438; G. Peruschi, *Informatione del Regno e stato del gran Rè di Mogor* (Brescia: P.M. Marchetti, 1597), p. 29; and V.A. Smith, *Akbar the Great Mogul*, p. 97.

103. Abu'l-Fadl, *Akbarnama*, vol. III, pp. 349-51.
104. G. Peruschi, *Informatione*, p. 29; and P. du Jarric, *Histoire*, p. 438.
105. Currently, it is an Indian city in the federated state of West Bengal.
106. K.S. Mathew, 'Akbar and the Europeans', pp. 117, 127.
107. R. Gulbenkian, 'Os quatro Evangelhos em persa da Biblioteca Nacional de Lisboa, o Grào Mongol, os Jesmtas e os Arménios', *Anais da Academia Portuguesa de História*, II Série, vol. XXV (Lisbon: Academia Portuguesa de História, 1969), p. 478; and K.S. Mathew, 'Akbar and the Europeans', pp. 117, 127.

2

The First and Second Missions at Akbar's Court

CHOICE OF MISSIONARIES

The Lusitanian authorities, far from being convinced of the sincerity of the emperor's intentions, viewed the diplomatic mission with distrust: they feared that the great sovereign had never renounced his plan to drive the Portuguese off the Indian coast. It was suspected, therefore, that the Great Mughal sent his men to Goa under the pretext of an embassy, in order to spy on the activities of the Europeans, especially when ships were arriving from Lisbon. On the other hand, the Lusitanians did not always respect the agreements stipulated in Surat in 1573: they often went back to imposing on the pious Muslim pilgrims who went to Mecca the purchase of passports, bearing, as we know, the images of the Virgin Mary and Jesus;[1] a reason that could arouse the anger of the orthodox Sunnites, who did not hesitate to ask the Mughal government for a decisive armed intervention.

Moreover, the request for some copies of the Christian sacred texts by a Muslim ruler could not but seem peculiar. The Portuguese of Goa, who knew the religion of Muhammad, were in fact aware that, according to the Islamic dogma of *tahrif* (scriptural alteration), the only Word of God is the Koran, so the Torah and the Gospel cannot be authentic because they have been falsified by Jews and

Christians.[2] Consequently, the reading and study of the Bible is strongly discouraged to Muslims, as useless or even pernicious activities. The Viceroy Dom Luis de Ataide[3] (1517-80) was therefore hesitant about the Great Mughal's unusual request and suspected from the beginning that he was only trying to attract Portuguese to his court who would serve as hostages if his policy of expansion into the Deccan led to a conflict with the *Estado da Índia*. In view of all this, the Viceroy of Goa was not to blame for his suspicions about the embassy, but since the Jesuits were not among the citizens directly under his jurisdiction, he was aware that the decision lay with the archbishop and his council and, therefore, avoided taking positions that could be interpreted as pressure. Three other bishops were present in Goa at that time: Matthew de Medina of Kochi, Leonard de Sa of China (Macao) and John Ribeiro Gaio of Malacca. The ecclesiastical council was in favour, because it was an opportunity to convert a powerful ruler and thousands of his subjects. The bishops' decision was communicated to the Viceroy, who forwarded it to the Jesuit Provincial Father, Rui Vicente,[4] for the selection of suitable missionaries, as requested by the emperor.[5] As a precaution, the staff of what was to be the first Catholic mission in Mughal India (1580-3) was not to include any Portuguese. After several consultations an Italian, Rudolph Acquaviva[6] (1550-83) and a Catalan, Anthony of Monserrate,[7] were appointed. Rui Vicente added an interpreter, Father Francisco Henriquez (1538-97), a Persian, Muslim convert to Catholicism, therefore a potential murtadd (renegade, apostate) who as such risked the death penalty.[8] Antoni de Monserrate, a 43-year-old Catalan, was commissioned to transcribe all his experiences in a diary.[9] Rodolfo Acquaviva, son of the Duke of Atri in Abruzzi and nephew of Claudio Acquaviva[10] (1543-1615), entered the Society of Jesus against his parents' will and, despite his health problems, was chosen for the Eastern missions, arriving in Goa just at the time of the arrival of the Mughal embassy.[11]

JOURNEY TO FATEHPUR SIKRI

The fathers prepared for the great mission with prayers and penances, taking care of the questions that could easily be raised by Akbar and the *ulama*. On 17 November 1579 the missionaries and the Mughal delegation left Goa: the Father Provincial embarked with them, accompanying them to Daman, where Anthony de Monserrate was waiting for them.[12]

Eight days after leaving Goa, the Jesuits arrived at Chaul and then continued on to Daman, where they stayed for four days before embarking on their overland journey (13 December). The Provincial Father and other Jesuits accompanied them for a few miles outside the city. The group spent the night in a village on the outskirts of the Mughal Empire and the next morning, after crossing the small river Parnera, the travellers entered Akbar's domain and arrived at Bulsar. The next day they reached Nausari, a great centre of the Parsees, in whose religion the Grand Mughal had shown great interest.[13] The Zoroastrians forbade touching the dead, so they were placed in towers of silence so as not to contaminate the fire, earth and water, which are considered sacred.[14] In fact, a Parsee learned with deep disgust that Acquaviva was carrying a casket containing a relic of St Stephen the Protomartyr.[15] The Jesuit explained that 'We do not carry about the bones of the dead, but of the living,'[16] so relics could be venerated. The Council of Trent had condemned the Protestant view that the cult of saints and relics was a form of superstition.[17]

The next stop on the journey was Surat, where the fathers had to stay for almost a month, as the ambassador Haji Habibullah did not want to resume the journey until the moon had reached an auspicious position (full moon). While waiting, the missionaries devoted themselves to the study of Persian, but they were frequently disturbed by visitors to the city, curious to meet these cultured foreigners so much in demand by the great and powerful Akbar. Many of them were impressed by the images of Jesus Christ and the Virgin Mary that the Jesuits displayed. Among these curious people there were still many Zoroastrians who held theological disputes with the fathers. But the latter were now impatient to leave to meet the emperor, confident that he would convert. Eventually (15 January 1580), when the moon reached a favourable position, the ambassador led the group out of the city, thus beginning a journey of more than 500 miles into the empire. The missionaries continued their journey in the company of a caravan of merchants, probably Portuguese or Armenians, who carried Chinese silk and other products to sell in the empire.

One had to travel with great caution, as unpleasant encounters could occur along the way: gangs of thieves and predators, especially in the mountainous parts of the empire.[18]

After leaving Surat, the Jesuits spent the night at Rander, on the north bank of the Tapti River, and the next day they set out immediately. Father Henriquez, being ill, was being carried on a litter and his porters, in their haste to reach a place to stop, had gone far ahead of the other travellers. Therefore, this first group met the governor of Surat, who had been ordered by Akbar to provide his guests with an armed escort for the passage through the mountains. While the governor was talking with Henriquez, his soldiers continued on, joining the rest of the company and, not realizing that they were the same group, the soldiers suddenly turned on them. Fortunately, the governor and the ambassador arrived in time to prevent a possible massacre, thus saving the lives of the fathers.[19]

After that the route for some time ran along the Tapti. The missionaries observed many Hindus performing their ablutions in the river, probably for the festival of *Ratha Saptami*.[20] Later, after passing Kukamunda and Tacoda in Khandesh, the troupe left the river bank and headed north-east, through beautiful valleys, rich in cereal fields and flowering mango trees. On 25 January they arrived at the city of Sultanpur, where the Jesuits stayed for three days to allow the ambassador to attend the Feast of the Circumcision of Isaac. During the night the fathers saw the graves of a Muslim cemetery and beyond the city walls they observed the solemn cremation of a body by some Brahmans.[21]

After Sultanpur the company marched through the difficult and perilous regions of the Satpura hills: the route was often so narrow that the camels had to be lined up and the carts pulled by men. The hills were also infested with bands of thieves, especially the Bhil, whose main occupation was to ambush travellers; in fact, they killed one of the ambassador's guards. Leaving the Satpura hills, the company crossed Surana and the Narmada River; two days later they arrived at Mandu, a well-fortified hilltop town, and from there reached Ujjain on 5 February, where the missionaries saw the body of an old Hindu being brought in a solemn ceremony for cremation.[22]

The team arrived at Sarangpur on 9 February, where Henriquez was received with great honour by many Hindus, as he was mistaken for a yogi ascetic. Finally, the Jesuits had the consolation of celebrating a mass. After crossing the Parbati River and the city of Pimpaldhar, the fathers and their retinue arrived at Sironj on 15 February. In the meantime, Akbar was regularly informed of the progress of the mission's journey through fast couriers. On 19 February the Jesuits encountered Mughal troops riding on horses, camels and elephants with magnificent trappings. These horsemen had been sent to welcome the missionaries and to escort them; their captain reported to Rodolfo Acquaviva that the emperor was anxiously awaiting them. Proceeding in a northerly direction the company arrived at Narwar, where the Muslims were beginning their *Muharram*[23] and the Hindus their *Holi* festival.[24] In this city Father Anthony of Monserrate fell ill, but, as Akbar was impatient to meet the fathers, he was left in the care of the ambassador's nephew. The others resumed their journey on 22 February and reached Gwalior two days later. The next stop was Dholpur, near the Chambal River, from where the ambassador led the missionaries directly to Fatehpur Sikri. Thus, after travelling for forty-three days from Surat, they arrived in the capital on 28 February 1580.[25]

INITIAL STAGES OF THE FIRST MISSION

The fathers were delighted when they entered Fatehpur Sikri and were received with all honours by Akbar, who stayed with them for many hours. The emperor wanted to offer them a large sum of money, but Acquaviva refused, stating that they could not accept because of their vow of poverty, as they were religious. The sovereign was astonished by the Jesuits' faith and praised them several times in front of his courtiers, ordering Domingo Perez to take care of his guests. Acquaviva was very pleased with the kindness and consideration of the Great Mughal and believed that this was proof of his imminent conversion.[26]

The missionaries were taken to a caravanserai, where Pereira was staying, where they were received the next day. They dined without meat, as it was the time of Lent, and after the meal, they discussed Akbar's attitude towards Christianity. Pereira said that the emperor had shown great respect for Jesus and the Virgin and even seemed convinced of the divinity of Christ. He was very impressed by the stories in the Bible, the chastity experienced by Christians, the law requiring monogamy and celibacy for priests. He still had difficulty understanding some of the mysteries, such as the Trinity and the Resurrection, but would have accepted them if he had been convinced that the Gospel was the true Word of God. He also listened to the account of Jesus' miracles and showed great interest. This information enabled the Jesuits to get an idea of the situation and to prepare themselves with great zeal.[27]

The first theological debates

Akbar had requested the Scriptures of the Christians, especially the Gospels, in his petitions; therefore, four days after their arrival the fathers presented the emperor with seven volumes of Plantin's famous Polyglot Bible.[28] When he saw those magnificent volumes, the ruler made some gestures in deference to the Holy Scriptures:

> He caught hold of each individual tome and, after kissing it, placed it on the head with great reverence in front of all his grandees and captains and the rest of the people gathered in the vast courtyard of the palace, and everyone was amazed.[29]

The Jesuit chronicler Daniello Bartoli (1608-85) informs us that the sovereign intended to compare the Bible and the Koran in a great dispute to establish which was the true Word of God.[30]

> Naturally the Jesuits had immediately accepted the challenge; for them not only the Holy Scriptures, but the whole apparatus of commentaries and scriptural interpretations constituted an intangible and unitary patrimony of truth [...]. Rudolph Acquaviva turns against the Muslims the ancient anti-Jewish argument, by means of which for long centuries of the Middle Ages the Christian Church had attempted to convert the Jews [...]: the New and Old Testaments are in full agreement in every part. The truth of the Old Law is confirmed by the New; the New merely develops the Old which prefigured it. Only Christianity enjoys this inner coherence, which is cultural and historical. On the other hand, no scripture has ever foretold the coming of Mohammed [...]. The real condemnation of Mohammed is the

cultural void that precedes him. The truth of Christ is not proven through miracles, but is recognized by all the Scriptures, even Muslim scripture.[31]

The Jesuits demonstrated their knowledge of the Koran, quoting several passages to support their arguments.[32] Acquaviva and his confreres had spent time on their journey studying Muslim culture, studying a Latin version of the Koran[33] and bringing with them a volume of Islamic law translated into Portuguese.[34]

During the same dispute, Akbar also asked the Italian Jesuit to read aloud some passages from the New Testament, whereupon an alim asserted, appealing to the dogma of *tahrif*, that there were quite a few prophecies about the advent of the Prophet Muhammad in the Bible, but they were deliberately erased, thus accusing the Christians of falsifying their holy book.[35] Acquaviva, with the support of Abu'l-Fadl, pointed out the absurdity of the arguments put forward by the *alim* and how there was no evidence to support the accusation of scriptural alteration against the Christians. The slightest alteration to the texts would automatically destroy the remarkable coherence that is characteristic of the Bible. Monserrate also accused Muhammad of misinterpreting Holy Scripture, suggesting that the Koran is a book full of historical anachronism, indicative of an arbitrary reworking of various biblical accounts by the prophet of Islam.[36] On the contrary, the Muslim thesis of an unlettered Muhammad with no knowledge of the contents of the Hebrew and Christian Bibles is intended to justify his lack of dependence on these sources and, above all, to attribute the text to God. On the other hand, for the missionaries, the sacred book of the Muslims had no revelatory character, because the possibility of identifying textual sources confirmed that it was not a faithful reflection of an uncreated Celestial Book, which is with God and which descended, taking the form of the historical Koran. As we shall see, the emperor himself had repeatedly questioned the Islamic dogma on divine revelation.[37] The Jesuits, now resorting to the classical method of medieval controversial theology, presented Islam as a veritable summa of the various ancient Christian heresies, which had long been condemned by the various Councils. The statements of the Koran were, moreover, largely already refuted in advance by the Church Fathers.[38]

The exposition of the Christian faith, however, provoked a violent reaction from the Muslim scholars, who turned the disputes into real fights. The emperor and Abu'l-Fadl generally favoured the Italian Jesuit and supported his views. However, debates became increasingly heated, and it was almost impossible to reach an agreement. Consequently, an angry alim suggested that God decide who was right: he would go through the flames with the Koran and invite Acquaviva to do the same with the Bible. Akbar was pleased and called Acquaviva aside: he wanted to make the Muslim burn. But the Jesuit refused to oblige, considering the plan infernal.[39] According to Palumbo's interesting observation, the emperor and the *ulama* believed that the supremacy of a religion over other faiths, that is, the truth of their God was proved, as the biblical tradition also taught, by the superiority of the miracles that God's envoy was able to perform. Even Christian preachers often stressed the importance of the charisms that enabled the Apostles to perform miracles to convert the Gentiles. But Acquaviva and his confreres were convinced that the miracle of the Apostles' time would never be repeated and, therefore, the missionaries had to base their successes only on their own strength and their ability to understand and communicate effectively. This scepticism about the miracle is the main reason why the father did not accept the challenge, seeking martyrdom instead. Acquaviva believed that crossing the flames with the holy book was a totally irrational act, since it meant imprudently defying the laws of nature, expecting immediate and above all useless miracles from God. The Jesuit did not accept the challenge not for lack of courage, as some *ulama* implied, but only because he did not trust in that kind of evidence.[40]

Akbar's cordial hospitality

Akbar always paid great attention to his guests, such as when he entrusted Monserrate to the care of his personal physician, Hakim Ali, as soon as he fell ill again and later decided to send him to Agra for convalescence. However, for a while the fathers had no opportunity to talk privately with the king and were therefore impatient to know his impressions on the progress of the theological disputes.

One day the emperor summoned them to the palace to inform them that he would soon allow Christians to preach freely in his empire and to build churches, convinced that no one would object, since he had already imposed himself on the orthodox Muslims when he allowed the Hindus to build their temples.[41]

On Holy Saturday, 2 April 1580, Father Acquaviva and his companions, with some Portuguese guards, left by Tavares, passed by the emperor to wish him a Happy Easter. Akbar received them with great honour and, after sending them all away, conversed with them all night. He asked many questions about Easter and the Resurrection, and also expressed his wish to attend the Christian rite. He also suggested that the Jesuits leave the caravanserai, where they had been staying until now, because it was too noisy, and offered them a residence in the palace itself so that they could meet them regularly and thus deepen their knowledge of the Christian religion.[42]

On Easter Day, Akbar had lunch served at his table and after the meal, the missionaries entered their new quarters, where they prepared an oratory, where they could retire to pray and perform their functions without hindrance. On the altar they placed an image of Jesus Christ and a copy of the icon of Our Lady known as 'Saint Luke', the *Salus Populi Romani*, which is in the Basilica of Santa Maria Maggiore in Rome.[43] Three or four days later, the king visited them and expressed his wish to see their oratory. He was very impressed by the image of the Virgin and honoured it with a deep bow. The missionaries thought that this gesture was a further sign of Akbar's interest in Christianity, but almost certainly the emperor was impressed by the pictorial novelties.[44] He immediately invited the court painters to study these 'exotic' works from the West to learn their style and technique.[45]

A few days later the Great Mughal returned to the Chapel with his gender, his three sons[46] and some dignitaries of the court, among whom was Abu'l-Fadl, who entered barefoot as a sign of respect. Father Rodolfo gave Akbar another painting of Our Lady that the Provincial had sent him as a gift; he took it with great respect and had it worthily placed in an important place in his palace.[47] The frequent visits generated great hopes in the fathers, who were always convinced of the imminent conversion of the sovereign.

The emperor placed great trust in fathers, entrusting his second son, Murad, to Monserrate to teach him Portuguese and good morals. The father took care of the boy, refusing to be paid. Apart from the prince, there were also other children at the new school, chosen by the emperor from among the sons of the high nobility. The Great Mughal often visited the school to see the prince at work.[48] It was probably shortly afterwards that, as Monserrate writes, at the beginning of each lesson, the pupils would begin to invoke the names of Jesus and Mary with devotion, to make the sign of the Cross and to kiss the image of Christ.[49] Murad, a diligent pupil, learned to read and write in Portuguese in just three months, thanks also to the collaboration of the sovereign, who made him repeat the lesson every day. Akbar is described as an affectionate but strict father: he gave Monserrate permission to punish his pupils, which initially frightened the little prince, but when he noticed the missionary's affability and patience, the boy soon gained confidence.[50]

The Jesuits and Abu'l-Fadl

In order to be more precise in their words, which the interpreter did not always render in their perfection and most adequate concept, the Jesuits asked Akbar for a good instructor to teach them Persian: the emperor entrusted this task to Abu'l-Fadl. The Fathers had a good relationship with him as he showed great interest in the Christian faith and, in the opinion of the missionaries, he, like his emperor, had turned away from the Muslim religion, although the Jesuits doubted whether he would convert to Catholicism. In any case, besides the emperor, Abu'l-Fadl and Hakim Ali also devoted themselves to the study of Christianity and its dogmas under Acquaviva's guidance. Sometimes, before theological debates, the fathers would inform the secretary of the sovereign of the topics they were going to deal with, preparing him in great detail and then being effectively defended by him.[51]

Rudolph Acquaviva, thanks to regular lessons, was able to express himself fluently in Persian within a few months and was therefore ready to contribute to the activities of *Maktab Khana*, collaborating with Abu'l-Fadl on the translation and commentary of the Gospels. As the Italian Jesuit writes, 'the king has asked us several times to translate the Gospel into Persian. As we feel this will encourage him considerably.'[52] In fact, the fathers had discovered that the Polyglot Bible offered, although the illustrations inside had exerted a significant influence on Mughal painting, was not exactly what the sovereign had requested, not only because he did not much like printed works, as we have learned, preferring instead manuscripts, but also and above all because he wished to possess a Persian copy of the Bible. This, we must remember, is an exceptional fact, since in the Islamic world there was and still is little interest in reading the Holy Scriptures of the Jews and Christians, who are accused, if one wants to believe the dogma of tahrif, of having altered the original message. Probably on the advice of the fathers, instead of the Arabic formula Bi-ismi 'llāhi al-Rahmāni al-Rahīm (In the Name of God, the Clement, the Merciful) with which all the Surahs of the Koran except the 9th are opened, Abu'l-Fadl used a Persian expression for his Bible translations, Ai nam i wai Jezu Kristu (Oh Him, whose name is Jesus Christ), somewhat unusual, because it does not use 'Īsā, the Muslim name of Jesus, present in the Koran, nor Yassou, the Arabic-Christian version of the name, but the Greek-Latin and Western appellative.[53]

Akbar changes his attitude

Disputes were held regularly, no longer on Thursdays, but on Saturday nights. Many topics were discussed, such as the Trinity, the divine sonship, the Incarnation, the Passion, Muhammad as the seal of Prophecy, the true Word of God (Bible or Koran?), the Day of Judgement, the Resurrection, etc. Due to his great theological training, Acquaviva confidently answered the objections of his opponents, who frequently complained to the emperor and Abu'l-Fadl about the alleged offences directed against their religion and Muhammad. On several occasions, the *ulama* again proposed the trial by fire and, when the missionaries refused, they accused them of cowardice. Acquaviva, in order to disprove them, said he was ready for martyrdom and proved it by accusing Muhammad as a false prophet in the presence of the emperor and the entire court. The Jesuit's intervention visibly angered the emperor, who begged the fathers to spare the Prophet of Islam from now on.[54]

The warning given by Akbar was, however, indicative of a change: at first, the Great Mughal's attitude had generated in the fathers' great hopes of a close conversion to Christianity, but after some time he seemed tired of the constant theological disputes. During the debates, he behaved like a fervent Muslim, appreciating the *ulama*'s attacks on the Gospel and taking offence at the fathers' insults to Islam. During lectures on the Christian faith, he yawned, slept and pretended to listen, or avoided them in order to watch the court jesters perform. Acquaviva did not hesitate to reproach the emperor several times for this sudden change, as well as for the contradictions of his regime and his conduct, especially against gladiatorial combat and his tolerance of bloody Hindu rituals, such as the *sati*,[55] which the Jesuit himself had been invited to attend.[56]

The emperor later informed his guests that he could no longer be at their disposal for a certain period and, therefore, they had to turn to Abu'l-Fadl or Hakim Ali in case of need. The Jesuits continued to attend to their duties, as when they celebrated the funeral of a Portuguese man who was in the service of the Mughal court, but above all they were able to translate further parts of the Gospel into Persian.[57]

In Goa, the authorities had serious doubts about the conduct of the Great Mughal: he would never convert and only used the Jesuits for political purposes. Acquaviva and his companions, on the contrary, felt they had good reasons to stay in Fatehpur Sikri. The Provincial Father, Rui Vicente, wished to obtain more information and, taking advantage of his visit to the north of the Portuguese mission, asked the Italian Jesuit to join him in Daman. Akbar, at first, agreed but, later on, did not authorize his departure, granting it only to Father Henriquez, whose presence was no longer indispensable, since Acquaviva now spoke almost perfect Persian. Henriquez was not well liked by the Muslims, who saw him as nothing more than an apostate. In order not to be recognized during his journey to Daman, he was forced to disguise himself as a merchant. He arrived in Goa in November 1581 and remained there until his death (1597). Acquaviva himself did not yet think it was time to abandon the mission, for which he still had high hopes, confidently awaiting the emperor's conversion. He therefore informed the Provincial of the reasons that led him to postpone his departure.[58]

The Kabul campaign

It is possible that the ruler's attitude stemmed from his growing concern at the rebellions that had broken out in several regions and the implacable opposition of some of the *ulama*, who could boast of the support of influential women in the harem. As a result, Akbar had tried to limit his meetings with the Jesuits and to conceal his interest in religions other than Islam.[59]

It seems that the main reason for the revolts was a general discontent with the centralizing policy of the Great Mughal. The process of centralization of power had undergone a strong acceleration towards the end of the seventies, with the reappropriation by the imperial treasury of lands given in *jagir*,[60] which were, in fact, transformed into *khalisa* lands, that is, under the direct administration of the emperor.[61]

Bihar and, shortly afterwards, Bengal also rose in revolt, to which Akbar promptly responded by sending the minister Raja Todar Mal Khatri, but without success. Subsequently, some groups of orthodox Muslims, who had been plotting against the sovereign for some time, because he was unworthy to govern an Islamic State, tried to replace him with a true Muslim, turning to Akbar's half-brother, Mirza Muhammad Hakim, Governor of Kabul, a pious Sunnite, but a mediocre man, politically weak and worn out by alcohol.[62] Muhammad Hakim, allied with the insurgents of Bengal and at the head of twelve thousand men, certain of the support of some courtiers and orthodox Muslims, left Kabul and advanced as far as Lahore, from where he intended to conquer Agra to seize the throne. However, the emperor quickly took matters into his own hands: he executed Hakim's supporters in his entourage, including Shah Mansur, the finance minister, and in February 1581 headed northwest, ordering his half-brother to return immediately to Kabul and submit to his sovereign.[63]

Akbar's army was three times larger than that of his half-brother and, in addition, was equipped with five thousand war elephants. Acquaviva wished to follow him in this campaign, exploiting every useful reason for his conversion, but he did not consent, above all so as not to give his adversaries any further pretext. However, the Great Mughal had Monserrate[64] accompany him so that Murad would not be deprived of his lessons during the expedition. Therefore, the Italian Jesuit found himself alone in Fatehpur Sikri, but he took the opportunity to perfect his knowledge of the Persian language and the Koran. Within a few weeks the king arrived in Kabul, from where Hakim had fled. The title of governor of the province of Kabul then passed to Akbar's sister, Bakht-un-Nisa Begum. With the order established, the emperor immediately set off for his capital. The emperor, who now felt very close in friendship to Acquaviva, asked him to join him in Lahore and resumed treating him with extreme kindness.[65]

The victory over his opponents definitively established Akbar as the undisputed ruler of northern and central India, free not only to express his religious ideas but also to continue the organization and integration of the empire.

LAST STAGES OF THE FIRST MISSION

When the emperor returned to Fatehpur Sikri, Akbar immediately had a conversation with Acquaviva, to whom he confided his attraction for Christianity, but also his perplexity about the fact that Christians worship three gods.[66] According to the Jesuit, the emperor was probably still influenced by certain Muslim polemicists, who accuse Christians of tritheism, unduly distorting or perhaps not understanding the meaning of the doctrine of the Trinity. So, he correctly explained to him the Christian dogma that God is One and Trine: Father, Son and Holy Spirit are one God in three Persons.[67]

After the Kabul campaign, theological disputes regularly resumed every Saturday evening. On one occasion, the *ulama* raised the question of the divinity of Christ, expressing their disapproval of a faith that considers the Mystery of the Incarnation. For Muslims, Jesus is only a prophet and a messenger of God and not the Second Person of the Trinity, the Son, who became incarnate in Mary's womb. The affirmation of the oneness of God and his unity is one of the cornerstones of the Islamic faith and the denial of the Trinity, although probably misunderstood by Muhammad, is clearly expressed in the Koran. The Incarnation is incompatible with the absolute oneness and unity of God: 'He is Allah, the One and Only! Allah, the Eternal, Absolute; He begetteth not nor is He begotten. And there is none like unto Him' (Surah 112: 1-4). The statement 'the Word became flesh' (Jn 1:14) cannot be accepted by Muslims: God is not subject to becoming, his absolute transcendence separates him radically from all created things. The missionaries argued, however, that the Koran itself in the fourth Sura, in coherence with the first verse of the Gospel according to John, uses the expression 'Word of God' to refer to Christ, allowing his divinity to be understood.[68]

Akbar and Abu'l-Fadl always seemed to agree with the fathers, but the orthodox Sunnis became more and more hostile and, consequently, the missionaries even more intransigent towards them. Increasingly tired of these diatribes, the sovereign gradually lost all interest in the debates and the *ulama*, decided to refrain from the meetings, which were, in fact, suspended from 1582.[69]

The conflict between the Mughals and the Portuguese

During this period the missionaries received reports of a conflict between the Mughals and the Portuguese for control of the north-west coast of India. The Mughals had never been interested in shipping; it was the Portuguese who held the monopoly and they never missed an opportunity to reiterate this. We also know that they had the exclusive right to transport Muslim pilgrims to Mecca.[70]

As we may recall, through a specially established ministry, the state granted a viaticum of Rs. 600 to each believer for fulfilling his duty as a good Muslim. However, in order to maintain the stability of the public finances, it was necessary to limit the number of pilgrims and, as a result, the orthodox Sunnis accused Akbar of wanting to prevent pious Muslims from fulfilling one of the five obligations of their faith.[71] When the Portuguese again demanded payment for the crossing from the pilgrims, the emperor grew impatient and in February 1580, just as the missionaries were travelling to the capital, he ordered Qutb-ud-din[72] to storm the ports of Daman and

Diu. After a long preparation, the Mughals of Gujarat attacked the Portuguese on 15 April 1582, but were repelled by the garrison of Daman and the Lusitanian fleet in front of Diu.[73]

The Jesuits were disturbed by Akbar's ambiguity, because he had not informed them of his anti-Portuguese policy, so they did not know how to act accordingly, torn between their loyalty to Portugal and their desire to convert the ruler. Because of the hostilities between the Mughals and the Portuguese, the Jesuit Provincial of Goa thought it advisable to recall the missionaries once again. But the missionaries, who always hoped to convert the Grand Mughal, tried to postpone their departure.[74]

Mughal embassy in Europe and the departure of Monserrate

In 1580 on the death of Cardinal-King Henry, Portugal had passed to the Spanish crown under Philip II (1527-98): Akbar realized that it was convenient to secure the friendship of the new ruler.[75] During the first half of 1582 he consulted his Jesuit guests several times to organize an embassy to Europe with the aim not only of achieving a resolution of the conflict but also of congratulating Philip II on his accession to the Portuguese throne and convincing him to join him in a league against the Turks. It was also the emperor's intention to send his greetings to Pope Gregory XIII, who, incidentally, probably at the request of the Jesuits of Goa, wrote him a letter[76] on 18 February 1582, in which he expressed his gratitude for the extreme kindness shown to the missionaries, but above all urged him to convert to Christianity.[77]

The embassy was to be led by a Muslim courtier, Sayyd Muzaffar, while Monserrate was chosen as his companion and Abdullah Khan with an escort was to protect them as far as Goa. They left Fatehpur Sikri in the summer of 1582 with a letter[78] addressed to the European authorities,[79] arriving on 5 August in Surat, from where they embarked for Goa. But no ship was leaving for Europe because of the headwinds and, therefore, the mission had to wait until the following year. Sayyd Muzaffar, who was not particularly enthusiastic about the idea of travelling to the West and travelling by sea, fled from the Portuguese colony and hid in the Deccan and, as a result, the embassy project was soon abandoned.[80] Anthony de Monserrate wrote a detailed report on Emperor Akbar in Goa[81] and in 1589 left India for Abyssinia, where he was captured first by the Arabs and then by the Turks and imprisoned for six years. Freed by payment of a ransom, he returned to Goa, and later went to Salsette where he died in 1600.[82]

Acquaviva's last period in Fatehpur Sikri

After Monserrate's departure, Acquaviva remained alone in the Mughal capital, taking up the post of tutor to the emperor's son, previously the task of the Catalan Jesuit. In a letter addressed to Claudio Acquaviva,[83] General of the Jesuits and his uncle, written before the embassy left the Mughal capital, the Italian father considered it advisable to stay in Fatehpur Sikri for several reasons. Firstly, he still trusted in the conversion of the king and his son, secondly, he thought it was possible to extend the mission to the people because they were good and well-disposed and, thirdly, the protection of the emperor guaranteed the possibility of moving freely in his empire. The General fully approved of what was reported to him, but unfortunately his reply arrived in India when Rudolf was already dead.[84]

Akbar continued to show great cordiality, but it went on without appreciable results.[85] According to Western chroniclers of the time, the Jesuit's last hopes were dashed when the ruler suddenly proclaimed himself the leader of a new faith in the summer of 1582. The Great Mughal would convene a great council in Fatehpur Sikri, gathering eminent personalities, including the loyal Abu'l-Fadl and Mubarak, to ratify the new religion, the *Din-i-Ilahi*.[86] The missionary, realizing by now that there was no possibility of converting the sovereign, resigned himself and expressed his wish to return to Goa. However, the emperor, who liked his presence and felt friendly towards him, did not allow him to leave and, in order to confirm his good intentions, gave as proof the fact that his son continued to be entrusted to his care. As a result, the father, clearly showing that it was impossible to convert Akbar, wrote several times to Goa to have him returned by insisting to the emperor. The Father Provincial, having been informed, finally recalled Acquaviva, who obtained permission after repeated requests and after promising that other missionaries would be sent in his place.[87] The Jesuit finally left Fatehpur Sikri at the end of February 1583, taking with him a family of Muscovites, slaves in the service of the Queen Mother, reaching Goa in May.[88] The missionary handed over a petition of the Great Mughal to the Provincial Father, in which he expressed his deep affection for Rodolfo and his wish to see him return to his court.[89] Acquaviva, however, was sent on a mission to Salsette with some brethren, where he was martyred on 27 July 1583.[90] The news deeply saddened the emperor, who is said to have exclaimed: 'Alas, Father! Did I not tell you not to go away? But you would not listen to me.'[91] The process of beatification began in 1598 and was only completed on 30 April 1893 during the pontificate of Leo XIII.[92]

THE SECOND MISSION

Akbar's invitation and the beginning of the mission

On 6 April 1590 a Greek Orthodox sub-deacon named Leo Grimon arrived in Lahore, the Mughal capital after the abandonment of Fatehpur Sikri.[93] He was travelling from Goa to his home country, accompanied by some Portuguese and Armenians carrying clothes and other products from China so valuable that they impressed Akbar himself. After being received with great cordiality by the emperor, who was immediately impressed by his culture and his ability to conduct interesting conversations, Grimon had the opportunity to talk about the Jesuits of St Paul's College, known for their preparation and prudence. Akbar, who at the time of the first mission had the opportunity to admire their theological skills, expressed the desire to welcome some religious of the Society of Jesus to his court again and the sub-deacon seemed to be the right man for a mission in Goa.[94]

Given the linguistic skills of his new host, Akbar initially preferred to commission him, with the help of a group of scholars from his court, to translate some Greek books into Persian, probably including the Gospels. When the work was completed, Grimon himself expressed to the emperor his wish to conduct an embassy to Goa. Akbar therefore provided him with a safe-conduct and a *firman* to be presented to Mirza Abdur Rahim, the governor of Gujarat, ordering him to provide the imperial delegation and the subsequent missionaries with an escort during the journey, indicating the route to be followed through the cities of Ahmedabad, Jodhpur and Multan and stating his responsibility for any damage that his guests might suffer.[95]

Leo Grimon reached Goa in October 1590, delivering further firmans respectively to the Viceroy Manuel de Sousa Coutinho, to the Jesuit Provincial Father Pedro Martinez, and to the College of St Paul, in which the Great Mughal declared his feelings of friendship towards the Christians and his desire to further deepen their religion. The Portuguese authorities were therefore requested to send other fathers who were willing to engage in theological debates with the *ulama* once again, so as to demonstrate not only the moral but also the cultural superiority of the Jesuits over the Muslim scholars. Akbar also ensured that the missionaries were free to return to Goa at any time, but if they decided to stay longer at the court, he would have Portuguese-style flats built for them. The emperor also donated a large number of precious stones and other valuables to the Holy House of Mercy, an association founded shortly after the conquest of Goa by the Portuguese in 1510, which offered assistance to the poor, the sick and orphans.[96]

After the failure of the first mission, the Jesuits were unlikely to be persuaded to organize a new mission: Rudolph Acquaviva's last letters suggested that it was impossible to convert the emperor. Leo Grimon assured, however, that the prospects of a mission were indeed favourable: the sovereign, in fact, was completely repudiating Islam; the minarets had been destroyed and the mosques used as stables;[97] Muhammad was as hated at the Mughal court as in the Christian kingdoms; unlike previously, boys over fifteen could now decide to be circumcized by their own will. The Greek added that Akbar had repudiated all but his first wife and had shown great respect for Christianity, even celebrating the Feast of the Assumption of Mary on 15 August 1590.[98] The news reported by the subdeacon was greeted with joy in Goa and the Jesuits were convinced of the importance of a new mission to the Mughal court. However, Leo

Grimon, in trying to persuade the authorities, had undoubtedly artfully inflated the facts to demonstrate the emperor's desire to convert.[99] As we shall see, a similar distortion of information also often characterized the letters that were sent from the various mission fields or from Goa to Rome to encourage new vocations.[100] In fact, the Father Provincial himself, who was particularly optimistic, wrote a report in November 1590 based on Grimon's information and sent it to the General of the Jesuits, Claudio Acquaviva, in Rome who thought it was time to convert Akbar.[101]

Towards the end of 1590, Pedro Martinez ordered two fathers, the Portuguese Duarte Leitao[102] and the Spanish Christoval de Vega,[103] accompanied by their lay brother Estevao Ribeiro, to go immediately to Lahore with Leo Grimon. During the journey, thanks to the emperor's safe-conduct, they were received with the utmost cordiality and kindness by the local authorities and in all probability followed the itinerary indicated by Akbar. At the beginning of 1591, the three missionaries arrived at the emperor's court without persecution and were received and hosted in his palace with all honours. The emperor asked the missionaries to start a school to teach the children of dignitaries and nobles, probably including one of Akbar's sons, and some members of the royal family to write and read in Portuguese. The fathers, therefore, at this early stage, in addition to participating in religious debates, devoted themselves to teaching, waiting for a favourable opportunity to talk to the emperor about religious matters.[104]

Given the promising start, Claudio Acquaviva was informed, albeit late in the day, about the possible success of the mission[105] and probably updated the Pontiff himself on developments. Pope Clement VIII then wrote a personal letter to Akbar on 17 November 1592,[106] but by then the mission had been completed for a year. In this letter he expressed his joy at the interest shown by the sovereign in the Christian religion, reminding him that Christianity is a revealed religion, founded by Christ himself, the Son of God, and that salvation is only possible within the Church. He therefore urged him to listen to the instructions of the fathers and to prepare for his conversion.[107]

Sudden conclusion of the mission

The emperor had been particularly busy during those times with the Sind, Kashmir and Orissa wars and had therefore had to interrupt his participation in the religious debates. He feared a general uprising if he became more and more helpful and accommodating to his guests, whom the generals and most of the officers, on the other hand, distrusted and disliked.[108] The missionaries found strong opposition from a faction at the court and soon perceived that the emperor had no intention of becoming a Christian and began to become disillusioned and to think seriously about abandoning the mission. The court nobles also claimed that the emperor's intention was to consolidate *Din-i-Ilahi*, of which he had proclaimed himself the founder and prophet.[109] Rather, the Jesuits were preoccupied with unsuspectingly collaborating with other exponents of the various faiths in the institutionalization of a supposed new religion. Likewise, the Sunnis were highly suspicious of the missionaries and thought that they were supporting the emperor in his religious policy. Leitao himself became convinced that Akbar was keeping them at the court solely to legitimize the new sect and soon began to suspect that *Din-i-Ilahi* was an entirely instrumental initiative to limit the influence of the Muslim community on the state; nothing more than a means to increase his own power.[110]

The missionaries therefore concluded that they were only wasting their time, as the king would never convert. But above all, there was a question of conscience: they could not collaborate with the emperor, nor give the impression of doing so. As the mission had been compromised, it was necessary to act immediately, and this is what Leitao did, without waiting for instructions from his superiors because of the distance and the slowness of the communication systems of the time, but consulting his brother Vega. So, in December 1591 he decided on his own responsibility to send Vega and Ribeiro back to Goa. The Provincial did not agree with the return of the two fathers: he hoped at least to send Vega back, since Akbar held him in high esteem, and wrote to Leitao, whom he ordered to remain in Lahore. But the letter was late and so Leitao, who left Lahore probably towards the end of 1591, arrived in Goa in early 1592, where he died of poisoning in 1593. Vega, on the other hand, after his return from the Mughal court, started working in a mission in Vasai and was later appointed Superior of the House of Chaul by the new Provincial. He died in 1600 in the Professed House in Goa.[111]

The emperor was surprised by the abandonment of the mission and in Goa this second failure caused great distress. In Rome, however, the possibility of converting Akbar was still being considered and the General disapproved of the departure of his brethren from the Mughal court, writing to the Superiors of India to appoint other missionaries.[112]

NOTES

1. J.S. Narayan, *Acquaviva and the Great Mogul* (Patna: Catholic Book Club, 1945), pp. 75-6.
2. According to Muslims, God revealed his books to the prophets who preceded Muhammad, in the same way that he revealed the Koran to the latter. These books are the Books of Abraham, the Torah revealed to Moses, the Psalter of David and the Gospel of Jesus. The Pakistani Muslim theologian Sayyid Abul A'Ala Maududi (1903-79) states that all these books, since they are supposedly sent by God, could contain nothing but the Truth in their original text.

   Of the books, we have been told, books of Abraham are extinct. David's Psalms, the Torah, and the Gospel exist with the Jews and the Christians, but the Koran informs us that these people have changed and interpolated these books. The Koran is last of the divine books sent down by God. The original texts of most of the former divine books have been lost, and only their translations exist today. The Koran, on the other hand, exists exactly as it was revealed to the Holy Prophet. In the former divine books, man mixed his words with God's words, but in the Koran there has been no such mixture (quoted in M. Hasan, *Sayyid Abul A'Ala Maududi and His Thought*, vol. I [Lahore: Islamic Publications, 1984], p. 84).

3. He was the Viceroy of Goa from 1568 to 1571 and from 1578 to 1580.
4. For biographical information, see J. Wicki, 'Vicente, Rui', in C.E. O'Neill and J.M. Dominguez (eds), *Diccionario histórico de la Companìa de Jesùs*, Biogràfico-Temàtico, vol. IV (Roma-Madrid: Univ. Pontifica Comillas, 2001), p. 3939.
5. V.A. Smith, *Akbar the Great Mogul*, p. 121; A. Mariotti, 'La prima missione dei Gesuiti alla corte di Akbar', in E. Fasana and G. Sorge

(eds), *India tra Oriente e Occidente. L'apporto dei viaggiatori e missionari italiani nei secoli XVI-XVIII* (Milan: Jaca Book, 1991), p. 80; and J.S. Narayan, *Acquaviva and the Great Mogul*, p. 76.

6. For more details on his life before and after his stay in Mughal lands, it may be useful to consult the following volume: F. Goldie, *First Christian Mission to the Great Mogul* (Dublin: M.H. Gill and Son, 1897).
7. For further biographical information, please refer to the book: J.S. Hoyland and S.N. Banerjee (eds), *The Commentary of Father Monserrate, S.J.*, pp. xi-xiv.
8. H. Didier, 'Muslim Heterodoxy', pp. 899-900; and id., 'Ormuz', pp. 164-5. There is little biographical information about Francisco Henriquez. We only know that he was born in Hormuz in 1538 and entered the Society of Jesus in 1556 in Vasai (S. Neil, *A History of Christianity in India*, vol. I: *The Beginnings to AD 1707* [Cambridge: Cambridge University Press, 1984], p. 171).
9. The Latin manuscript *Mongolicae Legationis Commentarius* was only finished by Antoni de Monserrate in 1600, shortly before his death, after several revisions. It was discovered in 1906 by Father W.K. Firminger in the Library of St Paul's Cathedral in Calcutta. Henry Hosten, a Belgian historian of the Society of Jesus, published it in 1914, with an introduction and notes (H. Hosten [ed.], 'Mongolicae Legationis Commentarius or the First Jesuit Mission to Akbar', *Memoirs of the Asiatic Society of Bengal*, vol. 3, no. 9 [1914], pp. 513-704). The English translation was edited by J.S. Hoyland and S.N. Banerjee.
10. He was the Fifth Superior General of the Society of Jesus from 1581 to 1615.
11. A. Mariotti, 'La prima missione', p. 80; E. MacLagan, *The Jesuits and the Great Mogul* (New York: Octagon Books, 1972), p. 25; V.A. Smith, *Akbar the Great Mogul*, pp. 121-3; and S.M. Burke, *Akbar: The Greatest Mogul*, p. 113.
12. F. Goldie, *First Christian Mission to the Great Mogul*, p. 58; A. Mariotti, 'La prima missione', pp. 80-1; and J.S. Narayan, *Acquaviva and the Great Mogul*, p. 80.
13. A. Mariotti, 'La prima missione', p. 81; and J.S. Narayan, *Acquaviva and the Great Mogul*, p. 80.
14. F.W. Clothey, *Religion in India: A Historical Introduction* (Abingdon: Routledge, 2006), p. 168.

15. J.S. Hoyland and S.N. Banerjee (eds), *The Commentary of Father Monserrate, S.J.*, p. 9.
16. Ibid.
17. Council of Trent, *Decree Concerning Purgatory and Invocation, Veneration and Relics of Saints, and on Sacred Images*, 3 December 1563.
18. F. Goldie, *First Christian Mission*, p. 59; A. Mariotti, 'La prima missione', pp. 81-2; and J.S. Narayan, *Acquaviva and the Great Mogul*, pp. 81-2.
19. A. Mariotti, 'La prima missione', pp. 82-3; J.S. Narayan, *Acquaviva and the Great Mogul*, pp. 82-3; and F. Goldie, *First Christian Mission*, p. 59.
20. A festival celebrated by the Vaisnavas on the seventh day of the month of *Màgha* (between January and February).
21. F. Goldie, *First Christian Mission*, pp. 59-60; A. Mariotti, 'La prima missione', p. 83; and J.S. Narayan, *Acquaviva and the Great Mogul*, pp. 83-4.
22. Ibid.
23. It commemorates the descent of the Koran from Heaven to be communicated to mankind.
24. It celebrates the arrival of spring by dancing in circles and with a shower of red dust.
25. F. Goldie, *First Christian Mission*, pp. 60-1; A. Mariotti, 'La prima missione', p. 83; and J.S. Narayan, *Acquaviva and the Great Mogul*, pp. 84-6. For a more detailed account of the missionaries' long journey, see J.S. Hoyland and S.N. Banerjee (eds), *The Commentary of Father Monserrate, S.J.*, pp. 4-27.
26. J.S. Narayan, *Acquaviva and the Great Mogul*, pp. 91-2; and A. Mariotti, 'La prima missione', p. 86.
27. F. Goldie, *First Christian Mission*, pp. 62-3; and J.S. Narayan, *Acquaviva and the Great Mogul*, pp. 92-3.
28. This Bible was expensively bound in gold and also contained illustrations engraved by Flemish artists of the school of Quentin Metsys, such as Pieter van der Heyden, Pieter Huys, Gerad Van Kampen and the Wierx brothers (Hieronymus, Jan and Antonie II). It was published in Antwerp between 1569 and 1573 by Christophe Plantin with texts in Hebrew, Chaldean, Syriac, Greek and Latin. The edition was patronized by Philip II (hence also called Biblia regia) and edited by the Spanish Arias Montanus (1527-98), chaplain to the monarch and a scholar of ancient languages. It was published in eight volumes and

not seven, as Daniello Bartoli asserts (*Missione al Gran Mogòr* [Rome: Salerno Editrice, 1998], p. 54), but since the last one was a glossary that was often not purchased, the Bible presented to Akbar must have been incomplete (C. Margolin, *Neuf années de bibliographie érasmienne, 1962-1970* [Paris: Vrin, 1977], pp. 403-4; J.S. Narayan, *Acquaviva et le Grand Moghol*, p. 93; A. Mariotti, 'La prima missione', p. 87; and G. Palumbo, 'La verità disputata. La missione di Rodolfo Acquaviva alla corte di Akbar tra passione per la parola e sfiducia nei miracoli', in C. Lavarra [ed.], *La linea Acquaviva. Dal nepotismo rinascimentale al meriggio della Riforma Cattolica* [Conversano: Mario Congedo], 2005, pp. 51-4).

29. A letter of 1580 written by the three missionaries to the captain of Daman, in J. Correla-Afonso (ed.), *Letters from the Mughal Court: The First Jesuit Mission to Akbar, 1580-1583* (Mumbai: Heras Institute of Indian History and Culture, 1980), pp. 29-30.
30. D. Bartoli, *Missione al Gran Mogòr*, p. 56.
31. G. Palumbo, 'La verità disputata', pp. 73-4.
32. Ibid., p. 74.
33. This translation, published in Basel by Theodor Bibliander in 1543, was the work of the English theologian, astronomer and Arabist Robert of Ketton (1110?-1160?), who, along with Hermann Dalmatian, Peter of Toledo, Peter of Poitiers and Muhammad—an obscure Muslim consultant whose name has been handed down only—was part of a group of translators to whom Peter the Venerable (1092-1156), Abbot of Cluny, had entrusted the task of translating important texts of Islamic culture into Western languages. An Italian translation of this version was published in 1547, but the missionaries probably did not possess it (S. Tramontana, 'Comunicare nel Mezzogiorno', in G. Musca and V. Sivo [eds], *Strumenti, tempi e luoghi di comunicazione nel Mezzogiorno normanno-svevo* [Bari: Dedalo, 1995], p. 23; and J. Correia-Afonso, *Letters from the Mughal Court*, p. 43).
34. F. Goldiė, *First Christian Mission*, pp. 66-7; and J.S. Narayan, *Acquaviva and the Great Mogul*, pp. 93-6.
35. Ibid., p. 97.
36. Ibid. Several scholars are inclined to affirm that the Koran does indeed contain various Judeo-Christian, biblical and especially apocryphal materials. Moreover, it is likely that the book is the result of a juxtaposition of texts composed during the period of the orthodox caliphs, based on Muhammad's teaching and cultural traditions in the early Islamic community.

37. H. Didier, *Fantomes d'Islam et de Chine*, p. 233; and M. Gallo, *Omelia arabocristiana dell'VIII secolo* (Rome: Città Nuova, 1994), p. 24.
38. E. Colombo, 'Jesuits and Islam in Seventeenth-Century Europe: War, Preaching and Conversions', in B. Heyberger, M. Garcia-Arenal, E. Colombo and P. Vismara (eds), *L'Islam visto da Occidente. Cultura e religione del Seicento europeo di fronte all'Islam* (Genoa-Milan: Marietti, 2009), p. 323; and L. D'Ascia, *Il Corano e la tiara. L'epistola a Maometto di Enea Silvio Piccolomini (papa Pio II)* (Bologna: Pendragon, 2001), p. 18.
39. H. Behr, *I moghul*, p. 136.
40. G. Palumbo, 'La verità disputata', pp. 62-4.
41. J.S. Narayan, *Acquaviva and the Great Mogul*, pp. 100-1; and F. Goldie, *First Christian Mission*, pp. 67-8.
42. Ibid., p. 68; and J.S. Narayan, *Acquaviva and the Great Mogul*, p. 102.
43. For a more detailed explanation of the icon, see P. Cellini, *La Madonna di S. Luca in S. Maria Maggiore* (Rome: 1943); M. Guarducci, *La più antica icona di Maria: un prodigioso vincolo fra Oriente e Occidente* (Rome: Ist. Poligrafico dello Stato, 1989); and G. Palumbo, 'La verità disputata', pp. 54-8. On the various images known as St Luke's and on those found in Rome, please consult F. Gregorovius, *Storia di Roma nel Medioevo* (Rome: Einaudi, 1966), pp. 350-1.
44. J.S. Narayan, *Acquaviva and the Great Mogul*, p. 102; A. Mariotti, 'La prima missione', p. 88; F. Goldie, *First Christian Mission*, cit., pp. 68-70; and G. Palumbo, 'La verità disputata', p. 55.
45. A. Okada, *Le Grand Moghol et ses peintres* (Paris: Flammarion, 1992), pp. 17-24.
46. Salim, the future empero, Jahangir, aged 11; Murad, better known as Pahari, aged 10 and Danyal aged 9.
47. G. De Filippo, *Beato Rodolfo Acquaviva S.J.* (Teramo: Edigrafital, 1999), p. 64.
48. J.S. Narayan, *Acquaviva and the Great Mogul*, p. 104; A. Mariotti, 'La prima missione', p. 88; and F. Goldie, *First Christian Mission*, p. 70.
49. J.S. Hoyland and S.N. Banerjee (eds), *The Commentary of Father Monserrate, S.J.*, p. 52.
50. J.S. Narayan, *Acquaviva and the Great Mogul*, p. 104.
51. Ibid., p. 105; and G. De Filippo, *Beato Rodolfo Acquaviva S.J.*, p. 65.
52. 'Letter from Rodolfo Acquaviva of 20 July 1580', in J. Correla-Afonso (ed.), *Letters from the Mughal Court*, p. 68.
53. H. Didier, 'Muslim Heterodoxy', p. 901; id., 'Les jésuites auprès du Grand Mogol Akbar', p. 20; id., *Fantomes d'Islam et de Chine*, p. 217;

S.A.A. Rizvi, *Religious and Intellectual History of the Muslims in Akbar's Reign with Special Reference to Abu'l Fazl (1556-1606)* (New Delhi: Munshiram Manoharlal, 1975), pp. 206-7; and K.A. Nizami, *Akbar and Religion*, p. 202.

54. P. Suau, *Les bienheureux martyrs de Salsette. Rodolphe d'Acquaviva et ses compagnons de la Compagnie de Jesus*, (Lille: Société de Saint-Augustin, 1893), p. 104; and J.S. Narayan, *Acquaviva and the Great Mogul*, pp. 106-8.
55. Suicide practice in the burning of a widow near the body of her husband.
56. P. Suau, *Les bienheureux martyrs de Salsette*, pp. 105-6; A. Mariotti, 'La prima missione', pp. 88-90; and J.S. Narayan, *Acquaviva and the Great Mogul*, pp. 111, 114.
57. A. Mariotti, 'La prima missione', p. 89.
58. J.S. Narayan, *Acquaviva and the Great Mogul*, p. 117; P. Suau, *Les bienheureux martyrs de Salsette*, pp. 110-11; F. Goldie, *First Christian Mission*, p. 81; G. De Filippo, *Beato Rodolfo Acquaviva S.J.*, p. 66; and L. Frédéric, *Akbar le Grand Moghol*, p. 262.
59. A. Mariotti, 'La prima missione', pp. 88-9; and J.S. Narayan, *Acquaviva and the Great Mogul*, p. 111.
60. The *jagir* or *jagirdar* system (i.e. hereditary fiefs granted to veterans) had all the political, cultural and economic connotations of a feudal aristocracy.
61. M. Torri, *Storia dell'India* (Laterza: Bari, 2000), p. 265.
62. A. Clot, *Les grands moghols. Splendeur et chute* (Paris: Plon, 1993), p. 102.
63. G. De Filippo, *Beato Rodolfo Acquaviva S.J.*, p. 69; P. Suau, *Les bienheureux martyrs de Salsette*, p. 112; and A. Clot, *Les grands moghols*, p. 102.
64. Anthony de Monserrate in his Commentarius offers a long report on the conflict.
65. G. De Filippo, *Beato Rodolfo Acquaviva S.J.*, pp. 69-70; A. Clot, *Les grands moghols*, cit., 102; and P. Suau, *Les bienheureux martyrs de Salsette*, pp. 113-14.
66. J.S. Narayan, *Acquaviva and the Great Mogul*, p. 134.
67. Ibid.
68. Ibid., p. 135; J.M. Delmaire and N.M. Zakka, *Jésus dans la littérature arabe et hébraique contemporaine*, Villeneuve d'Ascq, Presses universitaires du Septentrion, 1998, p. 20. It is true that the Koran speaks of the Word with regard to Jesus, but for Islamic theology Jesus is the Word of God 'only because his birth from a virgin mother is the fruit of

the creative Word of God' (M. Gallo, *Omelia arabo-cristiana dell'VIII secolo*, p. 60).

69. L. Frédéric, *Akbar le Grand Moghol*, p. 260.
70. H. Behr, *I moghul*, p. 136.
71. H. Didier, *Fantòmes d'Islam et de Chine*, p. 216.
72. Qutb-ud-din was the faujdar (governor) of Gujarat, son of Maham Anaga, Akbar's nurse.
73. J.S. Narayan, *Acquaviva and the Great Mogul*, p. 141; L. Frédéric, *Akbar le Grand Moghol*, p. 259; and H. Behr, *I Moghul*, p. 136.
74. L. Frédéric, *Akbar le Grand Moghol*, pp. 259-60.
75. P. Suau, *Les bienheureux martyrs de Salsette*, p. 116.
76. Regarding the letter, please consult J. Correia-Afonso, *Letters from the Mughal Court*, pp. 119-20.
77. J.S. Narayan, *Acquaviva and the Great Mogul*, pp. 141-2; L. Frédéric, *Akbar le Grand Moghol*, p. 260; and E. MacLagan, *The Jesuits and the Great Mogul*, p. 37.
78. A copy of the letter can be found in the first volume of the *Insha-i-Abu'l-Fadl*, a collection of Akbar's firmans compiled by Abu'l-Fadl. In the letter, trained theologians in Oriental languages and culture, and several copies of the Pentateuch, the Psalter and the Gospels in Arabic or Persian are requested (M. Haidar [ed.], *Mukatabat-i-Allami [Insha-i-Abul Fazl]* [New Delhi: Munshiram Manoharlal, 1998], pp. 8-12).
79. Philip II, probably also Pope Gregory XIII and the Jesuit General Claudio Acquaviva.
80. L. Frédéric, *Akbar le Grand Moghol*, pp. 260-1; and J.S. Narayan, *Acquaviva and the Great Mogul*, pp. 143-5.
81. *Relaçam do Equebar, rei dos Mogores* (H. Hosten [ed.], 'Father A. Monserrate's Account of Akbar', *Journal of Asiatic Society of Bengal*, vol. 8, no. 5 [1912], pp. 185-221). This report was the main source of knowledge about the personality of Akbar and his court, used by Jesuit historians such as Daniello Bartoli and Pierre du Jarric (1566-1617) (*Akbar and the Jesuits*). The contents of the *Relaçam* were later included in the *Commentarius*.
82. A. Mariotti, 'La prima missione', p. 81; and L. Frédéric, *Akbar le Grand Moghol*, p. 262.
83. Written in Italian on 25 April 1582, quoted in J. Correia-Afonso, *Letters from the Mughal Court*, pp. 102-4.
84. G. De Filippo, *Beato Rodolfo Acquaviva S.J.*, pp. 70-1.
85. Ibid., p. 71.

86. In reality, Akbar had not founded a new cult, but, as we shall see, intended to establish a sort of Sufic-inspired brotherhood at court.
87. L. Frédéric, *Akbar le Grand Moghol*, p. 261; and G. De Filippo, *Beato Rodolfo Acquaviva S.J.*, p. 71.
88. E. MacLagan, *The Jesuits and the Great Mogul*, pp. 39-40; L. Frédéric, *Akbar le Grand Moghol*, p. 262; and G. De Filippo, *Beato Rodolfo Acquaviva S.J.*, pp. 71-2.
89. For the firman, please see E. MacLagan, *The Jesuits and the Great Mogul*, p. 39.
90. Ibid., p. 40.
91. J. Correia-Afonso, *Letters from the Mughal Court*, pp. 123-4.
92. G. De Filippo, *Beato Rodolfo Acquaviva S.J.*, pp. 101-3.
93. Fatehpur Sikri was finally abandoned in 1585 in favour of Lahore, located in a more strategic area, i.e. close to the restive Afghan regions of the Empire and to the major communication routes with the West. Therefore, it is not the lack of water, as claimed by some scholars, that motivated the abandonment, but political considerations.
94. L. Frédéric, *Akbar le Grand Moghol*, p. 298; E. MacLagan, *The Jesuits and the Great Mogul*, p. 46; K.S. Mathew, 'Akbar and the Europeans', p. 121; and J. Correia-Afonso, 'The Second Jesuit Mission to Akbar', *Indica*, vol. 28 (1991), pp. 74-5.
95. K.S. Mathew, 'Akbar and the Europeans', pp. 121-2; L. Frédéric, *Akbar le Grand Moghol*, pp. 298-9; and E. MacLagan, *The Jesuits and the Great Mogul*, pp. 46-7.
96. E. MacLagan, *The Jesuits and the Great Mogul*, pp. 46-7; K.S. Mathew, 'Akbar and the Europeans', pp. 121-2; and L. Frédéric, *Akbar le Grand Moghol*, pp. 298-9.
97. The news of an alleged transformation of mosques into stables is also reported by Ionne Hay (*De rebus japonicis, indicis et peruanis epistolae recentiores* [Anversa: Officina Martini Nutij, 1605], p. 691), who further says that 'This king [Akbar] detests the Mohammedan sect […]. He ordered the demolition of all minarets and mosquees' (ibid., p. 702). Didier claims that 'what is suggested here to the Western reader is totally false' (H. Didier, *Famómes d'Islam et de Chine,* p. 321). We know that Akbar had only a few mosques destroyed that were not under state control and belonged to dissident groups. Contrary to what was thought in the West, the emperor had built magnificent mosques such as the Jami Masjid at Fatehpur Sikri in 1573 (ibid., pp. 210, 234).
98. A. Camps (ed.), 'An Unpublished Letter of Father Christoval de Vega S.J.', in id., *Studies in Asian Mission History* (Leiden: Brill Academic

Publishers, 2000), p. 49; K.S. Mathew, 'Akbar and the Europeans', pp. 121, 123; E. MacLagan, *The Jesuits and the Great Mogul*, p. 48; and J. Correia-Afonso, 'The Second Jesuit Mission to Akbar', p. 75.

99. L. Frédéric, *Akbar le Grand Moghol*, p. 299.
100. H. Didier, *Fantòmes d'Islam et de Chine*, p. 234.
101. K.S. Mathew, 'Akbar and the Europeans', p. 121; and E. MacLagan, *The Jesuits and the Great Mogul*, p. 46. For the Provincial's letter, see J. Wicki (ed.), *Documenta Indica*, vol. XV (Rome: Institutum Historicum Societatis Iesu, 1981), pp. 527-8.
102. Born in 1554 in Leiria, he entered the Society of Jesus in 1563. He was the Rector of Malacca College before being chosen as Superior of the Mughal Mission.
103. Born in Osuna in 1559, he entered the Society in 1576 and travelled to India in 1582, later becoming Superior at Daman.
104. A.S. Santos Hernandez, *Jeronimo Javier S.J., apostol del Gran Mogol y arzobispo electo de Cranganor, en la India* (Pamplona: Editorial Gómez, 1958), pp. 106-7; J. Correia-Afonso, 'The Second Jesuit Mission to Akbar', p. 75; E. MacLagan, *The Jesuits and the Great Mogul*, p. 48; K.S. Matthew, 'Akbar and the Europeans', p. 122; and L. Frédéric, *Akbar le Grand Moghol*, p. 299.
105. Towards the end of 1591, the Father Provincial wrote other letters to Claudio Acquaviva (J. Wicki [ed.], *Documenta Indica*, vol. XV, spp. 618-22, 639-45, 739-41).
106. For the Latin version of the letter, see J. Wicki (ed.), *Documenta Indica*, vol. XVI (Rome: Institutum Historicum Societatis Iesu, 1984, pp. 27-8.
107. K.S. Mathew, 'Akbar and the Europeans', pp. 122-3.
108. V.A. Smith, *Akbar the Great Mogul*, p. 184.
109. E. MacLagan, *The Jesuits and the Great Mogul*, p. 48; and A.S. Santos Hernandez, *Jeronimo Javier*, p. 107.
110. A. Camps (ed.), 'An Unpublished Letter', pp. 51-2; and J. Correia-Afonso, 'The Second Jesuit Mission to Akbar', pp. 92-3.
111. K.S. Mathew, 'Akbar and the Europeans', p. 123; E. MacLagan, *The Jesuits and the Great Mogul*, p. 48; A. Camps, 'An Unpublished Letter', p. 52; and J. Correia-Afonso, 'The Second Jesuit Mission to Akbar', p. 76.
112. A.S. Santos Hernandez, *Jeronimo Javier*, pp. 107-8.

3 Akbar and Religion

THE JESUITS AND THE CONVERSION OF THE GREAT MUGHAL

The Jesuits did not establish the mission in North India on their own initiative but at the invitation of Emperor Akbar. The friendly attitude and the interest of the sovereign in Christianity had generated in the fathers the hope of his conversion, which initially became the main objective of their stay at the court. In fact, they had sent several reports to their superiors in which they claimed that the event was imminent. There was talk in the West of the miracle of a possible and resounding conversion of the Great Mughal.

Distortion of information

As Didier observes, the information about the emperor that the Jesuits transmitted to Goa or Rome nevertheless has characteristics that are very close to the orthodox Sunni view of the ruler.[1] Many *ulama*, in fact, 'saw Akbar as a hateful tyrant who had turned away from Islam and even tried to hinder it; in short, an apostate [...]. The Jesuits took up and amplified the Sunni thesis that Akbar had denied Islam.'[2]

It was even suspected that 'he wanted to flee to Goa to be baptized and only the fear of a general insurrection prevented him from doing so'.[3] That the emperor had turned away from Sunni Islam is confirmed by numerous sources, but he never planned to convert to Christianity.

Some historians, such as the Frenchman Marc Gaborieau, argue that without a careful and cautious critical examination of the testimonies of European clerics and disillusioned Sunnis such as Bada'uni, one could conclude that Akbar was a murtadd (apostate); whereas it would be likely that he stayed within the limits tolerated by orthodoxy.[4]

The Indian scholar, Makhan Lal Roy Choudhury, without minimizing their historical importance, suggests that the Jesuit sources should be considered with great caution, criticizing above all their strongly apologetic tone; therefore, he does not give them much credit, also because, in his opinion, the Western missionaries were not able to understand the Indian reality.[5] Similarly, the Indian historian Sri Ram Sharma believes that the Jesuits did not fully grasp the religious and political situation of the Mughal Empire for several reasons: first of all, the difficulty, at least in the initial phase, to understand the Persian language, which may have caused many misunderstandings.[6] On the contrary, Didier asserts that the fathers were in fact linguistically and culturally prepared to frequent the environment of the Mughal court and understand the religious complexity of the country. Moreover, right from the start, they could benefit from the help of an interpreter, provided by their brother superiors and therefore a member of the same missionary group.[7]

Due to the continuous cultural, commercial, diplomatic and military exchanges between the Mughals and the Portuguese, the Goa authorities could have gathered quite a lot of valuable information about the court life in Fatehpur Sikri. It cannot be excluded, for instance, that they were already aware of Akbar's strong interest in European devotional art. So, presumably for this very reason, the Jesuits thought it wise to present some paintings with representations of Christian themes as well as volumes of the Royal Polyglot Bible, richly illustrated with numerous elegant Flemish engravings. In addition to illustrated books, prints and copies of Western paintings, the fathers of the third mission brought a Portuguese painter directly to the Mughal court with the precise function of teaching the artists in the imperial atelier the main European styles of the time.

As we shall see later on, the Jesuits, knowing that they had to deal with a certain iconoclastic mentality of Islam, were highly prepared on the arguments in favour of the permissibility of the cultic use of sacred images by Christians. We can therefore only agree with Didier about the adequacy of the fathers to the task entrusted to them by the Goa authorities, although great were the expectations and hopes placed in them. It does not seem appropriate, if not correct, to impute to these missionaries a cursory preliminary preparation, since they were requested—if we may say so—suddenly and unexpectedly by the Great Mughal. On the other hand, as we shall see, they were able to make up for their shortcomings by introducing new missionary strategies aimed at grafting the preaching of the Gospel onto the cultural and religious traditions of the place. Certainly, Jesuit sources, as current historiography rightly warns us, must be taken with due caution, but they are not the voice of someone who did not understand the reality in which they operated, rather they reveal the intention to arouse interest and satisfy the expectations of the West, often at the expense of the correspondence between facts and information disseminated.

The Jesuits at the court of the Mughals

> did not consider it necessary or useful to explain to their superiors in Goa and Rome all that they could learn about Akbar and his entourage, nor indeed about their own way of proclaiming Christ [...], because of a justifiable ignorance that their superiors might have had of the Mughal situation, certainly aggravated by the slowness of communications in India and even more so between India and Europe. For the missionaries it was inevitable, if not necessary, to have great freedom of initiative and individual experimentation.[8]

Moreover, as the scholar Zupanov argues,

> it is difficult to establish how the authorities in Rome managed and adjusted their strategies in the mission territories in India. Obviously the General of the Society of Jesus was constantly issuing orders and directives, but the implementation of these necessarily remained in the hands of the local structures. Even the most peremptory orders[,] for example those issued after the Council of Trent [...] were implemented quite differently in different places.[9]

Undoubtedly, the great distance separating the missions or

missionaries from the authorities in Rome or Goa, allowed a certain freedom in their decisions on the ground. Distance therefore had the effect of lengthening the time of the decision-making process.[10]

In general, insofar as they were intended to be copied or printed, i.e. to favour the arrival of reinforcements from Europe, missionary reports indicated that the conversion of this or that sovereign of a faraway country was quite possible, or even imminent, and that many bad news were being passed over in silence.[11]

Moreover, again in view of recruiting new evangelizers, it is likely that several documents transmitted by Jesuits on mission were edited and sent to their brethren in Europe, eager for news about India, misleading even the historians of the time who relied on these sources to describe missionary activities, not neglecting ethnographic data.[12]

At the beginning of a mission, but also during its development, a tendency towards optimism could, therefore, entitle one to select facts and even censor or distort them. Western chroniclers of the time, therefore, seem to have widely accepted the Jesuit thesis, ultimately the Sunni thesis, of an Akbar outside Islam.[13]

A miracle for conversion

Akbar always took care of his Jesuit guests with great kindness and courtesy, but above all he seemed to show a particular interest in their religion, raising in them, as we already know, the false hope of his imminent conversion to Christianity. The missionaries themselves, once they realized their misinterpretation of the monarch's attitude, tried to understand the reasons for their failure and questioned themselves on the real motivations of the Great Mughal to request and maintain a permanent presence at the court of a group of Catholic theologians.

According to the missionaries, one of the main reasons for their failure was probably the fact that they did not fulfil the emperor's request to see a miracle: several times he insisted that one of the fathers and one of the *ulama* enter a furnace, taking their respective scriptures with them. But for the Jesuits the period of miracles seemed to be definitively over. Bartoli writes, in fact, that God no longer puts 'in the heart of his servant that infallible certainty with which he always works who is moved by him to perform miracles'.[14]

Anthropologist Flavia Cuturi states that:

> during the modern season of apostolic proselytism, the missionaries soon had to realise that, unlike the Apostles, their intentions and actions were not accompanied by any prodigy or divine intervention [...] that would help convince the people to believe in Christianity [...]. The realisation of the solitude in which the missionaries had to operate had contributed to generating the notion of accommodation,[15]

which consisted in adapting the Christian message to the customs and values of the local cultures. However, these first Jesuits on Mughal soil mainly resorted to the method of *disputatio*, not only because it was more suitable to the situation, but also because the emperor had invited them to participate in the religious assemblies organized by him.

AKBAR'S RELIGIOUS POLICY

As we have been able to observe, the first two missions were interrupted by the fathers themselves, considering their activity absolutely inconclusive. Let us remember again that the purpose of their stay consisted above all, apart from other possible motivations, in the conversion of the Great Mughal: a conversion that, consequently, would also have favoured that of his subjects. This was certainly a remote goal, to be achieved gradually and prudently, but the Jesuits soon realized that the emperor had no intention of embracing Christianity. Rather, they feared that the Great Mughal was trying to amalgamate his subjects through the realization of a genuine spiritual unity in his state. In fact, in line with their fears, the fathers had understood his interest in the different religious systems to be aimed solely at the creation of a new cult: a syncretism resulting from the encounter of different faiths. Monserrate suspected that the sovereign intended to 'found a new religion, with matter taken from all the existing systems'.[16] Cristoval de Vega writes: 'It was obvious in advance that he called us in order to authorize the foundation of his new law with the aid of our presence and of other priests of false sects he had at his court.'[17]

Would the ruler have renounced Islam to adhere to a syncretist faith of his own invention? Did he want to merge an amalgam of all the religions he knew probably to unite all his subjects under one faith? This is a question long discussed in academic circles. Indeed, the figure of Akbar is still hotly debated today because of his complex personality, but especially because of the role and significance of religion in his life and politics. Today, it is generally maintained that the monarch had no intention of embracing any religion other than Islam, nor of adding yet another sect to the many that crowded the Indian subcontinent, but that he recognized himself in a Sufic spirituality. But in order to reach this conclusion, it is necessary to analyse the evolution of his religious policy in an orderly fashion, evaluating any influence exerted by his personal feelings and convictions.

The great Indian emperor, despite being the head of a Sunni Muslim theocracy, as an attempt to resolve religious tensions, had initiated reforms to ensure opportunities for religious practice for non-Sunni Islamic communities, but also (and especially) for non-Muslim.

Akbar had immediately sought to secure a stable and lasting rule over the whole of Hindustan, extending his conquests over the many surrounding kingdoms of Muslim and Hindu faith. Like the previous rulers, he initially behaved more like a conqueror than a prudent administrator in political terms, often imposing his own laws on the conquered populations without taking their culture into account.[18] The young ruler believed that peace could only be secured through conquest, arguing that 'A monarch should be ever intent on conquest, otherwise his neighbours rise in arms against him.'[19] However, having realized in time that Indian history had been marked by a succession of different administrations and ruling dynasties, from periods of territorial unification to periods of fragmentation, he realized the need to make a sharp change from the political line of his predecessors, if he did not want to inaugurate yet another short-lived reign.[20]

Akbar, a forward-looking ruler who was always careful to safeguard the stability of his power, soon realized the need to win the sympathy of the majority of the Hindustani population, who professed the Hindu religion. The Hindus, heirs to a millenary tradition, formed an internally closed community, organized according to principles of rigid social stratification into endogamous castes. The emperor was well aware that his Hindu subjects resented the rule of a dynasty that represented a small ethnic, religious and linguistic minority. After all, the Mughals were 'foreigners' in terms of homeland and faith and exercised their authority and power over a non-Muslim majority, whose members found themselves, paradoxically for them, resident in an Islamic state, with all the effects of not adhering to Islam, i.e. demoted to a state of legal inferiority (*dhimmi*). From the very beginning of his reign, the ruler realized the absurdity of maintaining a political and social balance in such a precarious situation, which could, in fact, at any moment lead to unrest and rebellion. Therefore, Akbar passed a series of laws aimed at the legal recognition of the Hindus, to whom he finally granted the free exercise of their cult and active participation in the public affairs of the state with the consequent possibility of being appointed to the highest economic, administrative and military posts in the empire.

A religious policy inspired by the Sufi principle of Sulh-i-kul

What were the emperor's real motivations for taking measures in favour of the Hindu population? Was he motivated exclusively by political interests? A careful study of the issue shows that Akbar's religious policy, which was indeed farsighted not only towards the Hindus but also towards other religious communities, was not only dictated by 'reasons of state', but was also inspired by an authentic and profound spiritual quest that absorbed much of his free time. Although scholars have often questioned the purity of his religious sentiments, we can, however, observe that since his adolescence the sovereign showed a certain inclination towards Sufic mysticism[21] and was particularly attracted by the thought of the Chishtiyya brotherhood,[22] whose mysticism was imbued with a very strong Ibnarabian monism, then opposed by Sunnism, which saw in it a denial of absolute divine transcendence.[23]

Akbar availed himself of the collaboration of eminent personalities of the time, including Abu'l-Fadl. The latter, a profound scholar and connoisseur of the works of Ibn Arabi, was an enthusiastic follower of doctrines that were heterodox with respect to the Sunnite belief system, above all an avid supporter of Sufi ontological monism, and exercised considerable influence on the religious policy of the Mughal Empire. In fact, probably thanks to his acquaintance, the monarch, certainly concerned above all for the stability of his empire, decided to adopt a policy inspired by the Sufi principle of *Sulh-i-kul* (Universal Peace) to definitively overcome the conflicts between communities with different religious and cultural traditions. This is a doctrine that preaches universal tolerance in religious matters and is based on a monist interpretation of the theory of *wahdat al wujùd*,[24] according to which God is the only one who really exists: God is the One Existing Reality, so that the world with its multiplicity and diversity of phenomena and the *Ego* with its individual experiences would have no consistency in itself. In this philosophical-religious system, therefore, a real difference between God and what we call 'creation'[25] is also denied, since the latter is rather an emanation or extension of God, destined to be part of the All, that is, of the One Reality. Human beings, in turn, also emanations of the One Existent Being, should aspire to unity.

The consequences of this type of monism on a more strictly political-religious level can be understood, precisely, through the concept of the *Sulh-i-kul*.[26] But the absolute tolerance that this Sufic theory flaunts can easily be confused with a certain relativism and with a conception of pantheistic syncretism: if everything that exists or, better, if everything we perceive, is an emanation of God, who alone exists, then man can worship Him by worshipping anything. Even the worship of the idols of polytheism would not be a practice that precludes us from meeting God.[27] Ibn Arabi himself did not consider idolatry objectionable, since the object of man's worship is God himself.[28] No religion, then, can claim to be the sole repository of truth: all religions are, in fact, on the same level, since they are all fundamentally expressions of the same truth, which is one,[29] and, therefore, can be compared to different roads leading to the same destination, but along the way are different from each other. At the same time, the *Sulh-i-kul* calls for overcoming the great variety of religious systems to achieve a kind of 'unity' in the image of the divine one, thus transcending any division of religions. After all, it can be agreed that, like the *dunya* (the world), *din* (religion) is a mere illusion, and so also religious differences, like all others, lose all significance.[30]

AKBAR'S ANTINOMIANISM

Akbar intended, through a reinterpretation of the very concept of 'Islam', to discover the essence of the 'true religion'. He was convinced that there was truth in every creed, hidden, however, by celebratory ritualism and mystified in rhetoric and ideological interpretations. The Great Mughal, in particular, rejected the extremely rigid vision of the *ulama*, who presented Islam as a set of religious and moral truths to be respected, believed to be based on divine revelation and Islamic tradition, a tradition that was binding on believers. We now know that the ruler drew on a certain Sufi literature that admitted and justified the existence of a plurality of ways to reach God. Therefore, also within the prescriptions of the Koran and the *Hadith* 'each man can develop the type of spirituality that corresponds to him. God uses a different language for each man, since each being is unique and responds to his own motivations, desires and possibilities.'[31]

The Sunni *ulama*, on the other hand, required the faithful to blindly imitate (*taqlid*) the conduct of the Prophet and the early Muslim community.[32] According to the emperor, *taqlid* was nothing more than a slavish obedience to tradition, a merely exterior observance of the cult, thus reducing Islam to a structured system of repeated rituals, a succession of instinctive and unconscious acts. Akbar, perhaps increasingly inspired by the universalist vision of the *Sulh-i-kul*, considered Sunnism, as well as the various Muslim and non-Muslim confessions, an illusory distinction from other religions, based on ritual diversification and a faith determined by *taqlid*.

For the Great Mughal, renouncing the Muslim religion based on imitation did not mean a rejection of Islam as such, but of its communal and ritualistic practice.[33] It is significant to note that in Abu'l-Fadl's writings the Islamic religion is usually not referred to by its name (Islam), but by the expression *Ahmadi-Kesh* (the Mohammedan doctrine), a *hapax* in all Persian literature. Akbar, who seems, by the way, never to have had the slightest intention of abjuring—or at least declaring to abjure—the Muslim faith, probably believed that the term 'Islam', meaning 'submission to the strongest', or rather 'to God', should be attributed to the 'true religion', thus emphasizing the relative character of the 'Mohammedan doctrine'.[34]

At this point, there was a clear awareness of the need to overcome the legalism of the ulama, to free man from religious preclusions or limitations. By this time, for the group of his closest counsellors, Akbar could embody not only the model of kingship, but also the ideal of *Insan al-Kamil* (Perfect Man or Universal Man), a term which, in Sufism, designates the man who has successfully achieved his spiritual realization, that is, unification with the fullness of the Divinity. The 'Universal Man' identifies himself with the divine will: he is free, therefore, from religious prescriptions, his intellect being informed by divine truth. In his spiritual reality, *Insan al-Kamil* transcends religious formalism, the practice of which he can follow, reject or adapt.[35]

The ruler in his spirit of *Talib-i Haqq* (free seeker of Truth) extolled the use of reason (*aql*) in religious investigations, giving full prominence to the *ijtihadi* before the *taqlid*. According to the emperor, for a religion to be valid, it could not contradict reason. During an inter-confessional dispute, he had, in fact, stated that:

> Most persons, from intimacy with those who adorn their outside, but are inwardly bad, think that outward semblance, and the letter of Muhammadanism, profit without internal conviction. Hence we by fear and force compelled many believers in the Brahman [i.e. Hindu] religion to adopt the faith of our ancestors. Now that the light of truth has taken possession of our soul, it has become clear that in this distressful place of contrarieties [the world]; where darkness of comprehension and conceit are heaped up, fold upon fold, a single step cannot be taken without the torch of proof, and that creed is profitable which is adopted with the approval of wisdom. To repeat the creed, to remove a piece of skin [i.e. to become circumcised] and to place the end of one's bones on the ground [i.e. the head in adoration] from dread of the Sultan, is not seeking after God.[36]

Therefore, as Bada'uni reports, the Great Mughal recognized 'acknowledged man's reason, not tradition, as the only basis of religion'.[37]

In a letter to King Philip II of Spain, written in 1582, Akbar clearly and completely condenses his thinking:

> As most people were prisoners of the shackles of uncritical acceptance [*taqlid*] without any real piety, they adopt the customs of their predecessors, relatives and associates that, too, blindly without any reflection, careful consideration and arguments. They accept the same faith among those whose followers they were brought up, and they remain without virtue of verification [*taḥqīq*]—a prerequisite of wisdom and truth—the finding of which is the proper goal of reason.[38]

The sovereign, who now disdainfully rejected instinctive faith in tradition, would finally declare that 'The pursuit of reason and rejection of traditionalism are so brilliantly patent as to be above the need of argument. If traditionalism were proper, the prophets would merely have followed their own elders [and not come with new messages].'[39]

THE RELATIVIZATION OF ISLAM

Akbar, who always intended to achieve in his empire a social reconciliation of religious differences or at least, if possible, to maintain a peaceful coexistence between confessional groups, planned a prudent but decisive religious reform, aimed at neutralizing Sunni Islamic radicalism, avoiding, however, the opposite risk of religious indifferentism that could derive from an extreme application of the Sufi principle of *Sulh-i-kul.* According to Didier, the emperor considered it desirable to propose and implement an attempt at Indo-Iranian adaptation of Islam, noting also the fact that the Indian Muslims had for centuries been immersed in a historical-cultural context, so distant not only from the ancient Arab environment in which their faith originated, but also from the Middle Eastern and Mediterranean environment of their contemporary co-religionists. Islam, like other religions, was but the product of a specific culture and a precise historical phase. In fact, it had emerged at the beginning of the seventh century in the Arabian Peninsula, so a renewal was necessary, determining first of all a process of de-Arabization, starting with the introduction of Persian both in the teaching of the Koran and in the sacred rites. There was immediate opposition from the Sunni elite, which aimed to safeguard the sacredness of Arabic as the liturgical language par excellence.[40] But nothing seemed to stop the Great Mughal in his attempt to promote a relativization of Islamic doctrine, an initiative that also seemed to imply a disavowal of the absolute and definitive character of Muhammad's prophecy. The emperor in his many close meetings with exponents of the different religions was above all looking for arguments against Muslim traditionalism. It is in this context that the role of the Jesuits can be placed.

THE CONTRIBUTION OF THE JESUITS

In the past, several historians have stated that the reasons why Akbar requested some Christian theologians were mostly foreign policy: the sovereign considered the presence of the fathers at the court as a valid means to maintain and improve his not always happy relations with the Portuguese power, which included not only trade relations between the Empire and the Middle East and Africa, but also the pilgrimage to Mecca. Matthew Ricci, who was in Goa at the time, was able to express in a letter dated 1 December 1581, written in a very good Portuguese, a judgement on the situation: Akbar would have invited some missionaries to his court not only to satisfy his curiosity in religious matters, but also to live in peace and good relations with the Portuguese.[41] Akbar feared that the Portuguese might obstruct the route of ships travelling from the Gujarat coast to the Middle East and wanted merchants from various parts of the world to be able to reach his empire without any problems.[42]

It can be assumed, however, that the intentions of the fathers were mainly spiritual and did not entertain the idea of exerting an influence on the Mughal court to the benefit of the interests of the Lusitanians. It might well be recalled, for instance, that none of the Jesuits of the first mission were Portuguese,[43] although this does not exclude that these missionaries were also placed under the protection of the Portuguese of Goa, for they were in fact requested by the emperor to the viceroy.[44] The Lusitanian government initially tended to favour its own compatriots, excluding preachers of other nationalities; but, since the number of missionaries that Portugal could provide for its vast colonies was insufficient, foreigners were soon admitted as well. However, all non-Portuguese missionaries destined for Asian lands were expected to sail from Lisbon, even imposing a compulsory stay in Portugal before obtaining a passport. The Jesuits also operated within the boundaries set at the Padroado by the Pope; however, they could escape the political and religious jurisdiction of the Lusitanians, not only because they often acted outside the direct territorial domain, but also because, according to their Constitution, they depended directly on the Pope and their Order.[45]

Some scholars have asserted that the Great Mughal hosted Christian scholars at his court simply because he liked the presence of men of different nationalities, especially learned men, at the palace in order to increase the prestige and splendour of his court.[46] The orientalist Giuseppe Tucci writes: 'The great emperor and his immediate successors, overcoming the stubborn resistance of the suspicious and distrustful court, opened the doors to foreigners and their culture.'[47] Authors often allude in particular to his keen interest in comparative religions:

> The fact that Akbar had always been very curious about religious matters is something that everyone acknowledges; it was precisely for this reason that he invited the Jesuits to his court. The Jesuits were but representatives of one of the many religious faiths in which he had been interested during his life [...]. They had all communicated interesting religious experiences. Experiences that he now wanted to use for a specific political project. What he now wanted to know was whether, hidden within the pages of one of the many sacred books in which the sages placed their trust, there might be the final word to satisfy his long-standing curiosity. His curiosity about the Christian Holy Scriptures was part of his great thirst for knowledge.[48]

Certainly, a comparison between different religious systems would not only have led to mutual enrichment, but for Akbar it would also have allowed him to highlight any similarities between them, potentially offering a secure basis for the search for truth. However, it seems that the presence of Catholic theologians at the court had a very specific purpose: to provide serious arguments against the traditional Islamic hermeneutics. Akbar, in fact, was not really interested in any demonstration of the validity of Christianity, in positive considerations about this religion, but in the armamentarium of Western anti-Islamic polemics. In the theological disputes, the fathers found in the *ulama* very convinced opponents who, in turn, largely took up the classical arguments of the Islamic anti-Christian polemic: in particular the accusation of the *tahrif* of the Scriptures and the doctrines of the Trinity and the Incarnation, perceived as blatant contradictions, respectively, of the divine Oneness and Transcendence. The Fathers, however, demonstrated their competence and preparation on the subjects they dealt with, standing up to their rivals, and thus had the opportunity to demonstrate their great capacity for argument. Above all, they revealed a great deal of sagacity in uncovering anomalies and inconsistencies among the statements of the Koran. As we can recall, for the Jesuits, in addition to the Holy Scriptures, the whole apparatus of scriptural commentaries and interpretations formed a unique patrimony of truth. 'It was from the internal coherence of this cultural and historically verifiable heritage that they drew the persuasive force of their missionary method.'[49] It was on this terrain that they fought their battles against the *ulama*, who challenged that coherence,[50]

> unlike the ancient missionaries who, in similar situations, had not drawn from this heritage the persuasive force to be used with 'infidels and idolaters', but had more 'scholastically' adhered to an abstractly philosophical model of dispute, and had inspired their action solely by the power of the Spirit of God according to the image of Pentecost. Strengthened also by the experience of the earlier failures of so many missionaries, the Jesuits were at ease in these great cultural battles.[51]

Akbar, therefore, could hope to find in the fathers allies capable of refuting certain truths considered unquestionable, in particular the definitiveness of Muhammad's prophecy and the insuperability of the Islamic sacred text.

MUHAMMAD AND THE KORAN

As we remember, for reasons of political balance and personal prestige, Akbar intended to become the sole leader of his Muslim subjects, and for this reason he met with strong opposition from the Sunni *ulama*, but he cleverly managed to limit their power, preventing them from interfering in state affairs. In organizing the theological debates, the ruler was already aiming to break their prestige and influence acquired in previous eras. The fact that bitter differences remained between them could be a pretext to set himself up as the legislator of religious society in their place and to demonstrate that all the measures he adopted were not contrary to Islam, but to some historically obsolete interpretations. Not only that, but the sovereign, claiming a direct personal relationship with the deity, could now dispense with the intercession of any religious mediator.

Claiming for himself the title of caliphate and on the basis of a theocratic conception of the state, the emperor arrogated to himself the right to govern in the name of God and to legislate also in religious matters, a faculty which, according to tradition, was granted to Muhammad, the seal of the total and definitive revelation of Allah for the majority of Islamic currents. The Great Mughal and intimates believed that prophecy did not end with Muhammad, but that other men were called upon to carry out a prophetic mission, by virtue of their divine proximity. Therefore, the court carried out extensive propaganda with the aim of affirming Akbar's superiority over the Prophet, wanting to arouse in the subjects the idea that the sovereign was the object of a particular divine predilection, due to his celestial origin.

The court also became a sort of residual space where it was easier to cultivate perplexity and scepticism towards truths that seemed indisputable for centuries, such as the dogma according to which the Koran was dictated by God to Muhammad through the angel Gabriel. In reality, as is well known, there are many concordances and relations between the Bible and the Koran and, therefore, the hypothesis of a dependence, at least in part, of the latter on the former would be acceptable.[52] However, in the Islamic tradition, the divine origin of the Koran is out of the question, because it would be nothing more than the transmission, faithful though partial, of a celestial archetype coeternally present with God, called *Umm al-Kitab* (Mother of the Book), which is also the prototype of all revelation, such as that contained in the Torah, Psalms and Gospel;

but in their original tenor, not in the texts currently possessed by Jews and Christians. The Koran, therefore, is not the culmination of the revelations to the Jewish and Christian faithful of antiquity, nor was it elaborated from earlier scriptures, which would have undergone alterations and interpolations, but it came down immediately from God, in its completed form, and is the reflection of the celestial archetype.[53]

The authenticity of the Koranic revelation would be somehow corroborated by the thesis of Muhammad's illiteracy. The term *Al-nabi al-'ummi* means 'unlettered prophet', in the sense that he did not know the Scriptures, i.e. heathen, before receiving the Revelation.[54] Therefore, the expression would indicate Muhammad's total lack of knowledge of the contents of the Hebrew and Christian Bible,[55] thus further supporting the uniqueness and truthfulness of divine revelation.

According to Didier, Akbar and his closest courtiers, increasingly committed to establishing religion on a rational basis, could not accept the idea that the Koran was a copy of a heavenly book dictated to the Prophet by the angel Gabriel at God's behest. The Koran would not be a revealed book, but a human book, whose wisdom would rather reveal its inspired nature. Therefore one could not exclude the recognition of an influence of other monotheistic religions such as Judaism and Christianity[56] that were present in the Arabian Peninsula.[57]

The sovereign, however, did not hope for the abolition of the Islamic faith, but for its development, especially in terms of overcoming mythical elements: a faith purged of all irrational elements, which no longer sought to continually subvert man's logical certainties.

In the past, scholars have often supported the following thesis: Akbar abandoned Islam to adopt a religion of his own invention, a sort of rationalist syncretism, the so-called *Din-i-Ilahi* (Divine Religion) or *Tawhid-i-Ilahi* (Divine Monotheism, or Divine Oneness). In reality, the Great Mughal, who in his heart always remained attached to a Sufic spirituality, had not conceived the plan to establish a new cult, but, as we know, influenced by the heterodox tendencies of the Indian Muslim environment, aimed at a reform of Islam. *Din-i-Ilahi* would rather be reminiscent of a small circle of the emperor's intimates, like disciples gathered around a master, similar to a Sufic brotherhood. Moreover, as the historian Eraly points out, 'Din Ilahi was not for the masses': the ruler was reluctant 'to initiate indiscriminately all who wanted to join the fraternity', who 'was frankly elitist'.[58] According to the Italian orientalist Alberto Ventura, *Din-i-Ilahi* 'presents us with an extremely aristocratic character, which has nothing to do with the tolerance and religious indifference to which it is being reduced'.[59] In any case, as the prince and scholar Frederick Christian Karl Augustus von Noer (1830-81) already stated, *Din-i-Ilahi* was above all important from a practical point of view:

> it was a political fraternity the members of which had bound themselves by oath to stand by the emperor in good and ill-fortune, in joy and in trouble. The wow was faithfully performed; Akbar was able to rely upon them when in later times his sons caused him bitter heart-ache.[60]

Akbar's heterodox ideas attracted the vindictive scorn of the Sunni *ulama* (and others), among whom many assured their support to the feudal aristocracy, increasingly worried about the emperor's policy of centralization. There was no lack, therefore, of revolts, conspiracies and attempts at rebellion which, although they were always repressed, served to make the Great Mughal understand that the time was still too early to propose a religious reform in his empire; a reform which in reality also contained strong political and social implications. Akbar, consequently, had to abandon his dream of a pan-Indian state, in which the entire population would be united by a single cultural and linguistic identity, even though among his many objectives there was probably also the sincere aim of promoting greater social cohesion. The sovereign, in fact, soon realized that forcing further the coexistence of such heterogeneous and, at the same time, equally hostile groups would have undermined the minimum social balance, painstakingly achieved, an important factor in ensuring political stability and therefore necessary not to compromise the security of the throne.

Religious policy was always a fundamental aspect of Akbar's rule. One of his main concerns was to be recognized as the sovereign by all the people subject to him, regardless of their religious affiliation. We know that in order to enjoy greater popularity among his non-

Muslim subjects, who represented the majority of the population, the Great Mughal had progressively started a series of important cultural and religious reforms and various measures to remove any ethnic or religious discrimination. We still remember his audacious intention to strip Sunnism of the privilege of being the state religion, in order to promote rather an adaptation of Islam to Indian religious pluralism. All this was certainly for reasons of political order and personal power, but it also corresponded, we repeat, to the emperor's personal ideas, which were the fruit of a long and authentic spiritual quest. We can therefore conclude this chapter by affirming that in Akbar it was not only the 'man of government' who conditioned the choices of religious policy, but also his own religious convictions, which depended heavily on the influence of heterodox Islamic currents.

NOTES

1. H. Didier, *Fantòmes d'Islam et de Chine,* p. 213.
2. Ibid., pp. 211-12.
3. Ibid., p. 212.
4. M. Gaborieau, 'Akbar et la construction de l'empire (1556-1605)', in C. Markovits (ed.), *Histoire dell'Inde moderne. 1480-1950* (Lille: Fayard, 1994), pp. 109, 113.
5. M.L. Roy Choudhury, *The Din-i-Ilahi or the Religion of Akbar*, pp. 105-8.
6. S.R. Sharma, *The Religious Policy of the Mughal Emperors* (New Delhi: Munshiram Manoharlal, 1988), p. 46.
7. H. Didier, 'Les jésuites auprès du Grand Mogol Akbar', pp. 26-7.
8. Id., *Fantomes d'Islam et de Chine,* pp. 209, 211.
9. I.G. Zupanov, 'Correnti e controcorrenti. La geopolitica gesuita in Asia (XVI secolo)', in P. Broggio, F. Cantù, P.A. Fabre and A. Romano (eds), *I gesuiti ai tempi di Claudio Acquaviva. Strategie politiche, religiose e culturali tra Cinque e Seicento* (Brescia: Morcelliana, 2007), p. 208.
10. Ibid., p. 212.
11. H. Didier, *Fantomes d'Islam et de Chine*, p. 213.
12. Ibid., p. 210. Didier also states that in the case of other Jesuit missions, among the factors distorting information, it is likely that there was also the need not to draw attention to certain missionary practices that were so divergent from those of countries of ancient and consolidated Christianity, such as disguising oneself as a merchant in order to pass

unobserved or as an adept of other religions, and the translation of the Bible and liturgical books into local languages, which provoked vehement controversy and scandal because of the danger of forms of syncretism, even though it was clear that they were instrumental in bringing the people closer to Catholicism (ibid., p. 234).

13. Ibid., p. 213.
14. D. Bartoli, *Missione al Gran Mogòr*, p. 74.
15. F. Cuturi, 'Introduzione. Adattarsi, modellare e convertire', in id. (ed.), *In nome di Dio. L'impresa missionaria di fronte all'alterità* (Rome: Meltemi, 2004), p. 24.
16. J.S. Hoyland and S.N. Banerjee (eds), *The Commentary of Father Monserrate,* p. 184.
17. A letter of 2 December 1593, quoted in A. Camps, *Studies in Asian Mission History*, p. 51.
18. L. Frédéric, *Akbar le Grand Moghol*, p. 88.
19. Abu'l-Fadl, *Ain-i-Akbari*, vol. III, p. 399.
20. L. Frédéric, *Akbar le Grand Moghol*, p. 88.
21. According to his principal chronicler, Abu'l-Fadl, as early as 1557, the young ruler, at the age of 15, had an experience of religious ecstasy, when, during the siege of Mankot, as if driven by a strong impulse, he went into the desert to get away 'from the presence of short-sighted men' who were troubling him (Abu'l-Fadl, *Ain-i-Akbari*, quoted in A. Eraly, *Emperors of the Peacock Throne*, p. 183).
22. The *tariqa* (brotherhood) of the Chishtiyya was founded by Abu Ishaq Shami (d. 940), who, at the invitation of his spiritual master Khwadja Mamshad Ulw of Dinawar, spread the ideals of Sufism in the city of Chishti (hence the name Chishtiyya), some 60 miles east of Herat in what is now western Afghanistan. It was then Muin-ud-din Chishti (1141-1236) who, towards the end of the twelfth century, settled in Ajmer, south-west of Delhi, and introduced the *tariqa* in India, gaining a great following both among the Muslims and the Hindus, as he proposed a less legalistic Islam, syncretically adopting some elements extrapolated from the native religions: the Chishtiyya became, therefore, the main Sufi order of the peninsula (K.A. Nizami, 'Cishtiyya', in P.J. Bearman, T. Bianquis, C.E. Bosworth, E. Van Donzel and W.P. Heinrichs [eds], *Encyclopédie de l'Islam*, vol. II, pp. 51-7).
23. Until the middle of the fourteenth century, the Indian Sufis were mainly limited to teaching piety in line with the fundamental principles of Islam. But later on, the cosmological and metaphysical doctrines of the Andalusian mystic Ibn Arabi (1165-1240) began to spread in

some Indian orders (D. Matringe, *Un Islam non arabe*, p. 138) and, being susceptible to various different interpretations, could perfectly fit in with the mystical theories of Hinduism and other Indian religious movements. The theory of *wahdat al wujùd* (Oneness of Being), according to which the being of the creature is nothing but the Divine Being, ended up being considered as a form of ontological monism, whereby there is in fact nothing in existence but the unique Being of God; many Indian Sufic currents, consequently, acquired a monistic connotation, emphasizing the oneness of God and attenuating, perhaps also due to a certain influence of the Vedanta school, the detachment of the creature from the Creator (H. Didier, 'Muslim Heterodoxy', pp. 926-7). For further information on Ibn Arabi and his writings, see the following texts: C. Addas, *Ibn Arabi ou la quète du soufre rouge* (Paris: Gallimard, 1989); M. Chodkiewicz, *Le Sceau des Saints, Prophétie et Sainteté dans la doctrine d'Ibn 'Arabî* (Paris: Gallimard, 1986).

24. H. Didier, 'Muslim Heterodoxy', p. 926.
25. Ibid.
26. I.A. Khan, 'Akbar's Personality Traits and World Outlook: A Critical Reappraisal', in I. Habib (ed.), *Akbar and His India* (New Delhi: Oxford University Press, 1997), p. 88; and I. Habib, 'Introduction: Commemorating Akbar', in I.A. Khan (ed.), *Akbar and His Age*, pp. xii-xiii.
27. H. Didier, 'Muslim Heterodoxy', p. 926.
28. The Andalusian mystic asserted that the Prophet Muhammad, in his condemnation of idolatry, was referring in particular to the form of worship of the common people and their ignorance of Reality. In the language of the poets Ibn Arabi wrote:

    O marvel! A garden amidst fires! / My heart has become capable of every form: it is a pasture for gazelles and a convent for Christian monks / And a temple for idols and the pilgrim's Ka'ba and the tables of the Tora and the book of the Koran / I follow the religion of Love: whatever way Love's camels take, that is my religion and my faith (Ibn Arabi, *The Interpreter of Desires*, quoted in I.Y. Junghare, *Topics In Pali Historical Phonology* [Delhi: Motilal Banarsidass, 2008], pp. 68-9).

29. A. Agrawal, *Studies in Mughal History* (Delhi: Motilal Banarsidass, 1983), p. 126.
30. S. Moosvi, 'The Road to Sulh-i Kul: Akbar's Alienation from Theological Islam', in I. Habib (ed.), *Religion in Indian History* (New Delhi: Tulika Books, 2010), p. 173; and I. Habib, 'Introduction: Commemorating Akbar', pp. xii-xiii.

31. P. Ringgenberg, *L'univers symbolique des arts islamiques* (Paris: L'Harmattan, 2009), p. 490.
32. G. Aneer, *Akbar the Great Mogul and his Religious Thoughts* (Uppsala: Skriv Service AB, 1973), p. 81.
33. Ibid., pp. 81-2.
34. M. Athar Ali, *Mughal India*, p. 162.
35. G. Aneer, *Akbar the Great Mogul*, pp. 62-6.
36. Abu'l-Fadl, *Akbarnama*, vol. III, p. 369.
37. Bada'uni, *Muntakhab al-Tawarikh*, in A. Eraly, *Emperors of the Peacock Throne*, p. 193.
38. M. Haidar (ed.), *Mukatabat-i-Al-lami [Insha-i-Abul Fazl]*, pp. 9-10.
39. Abu'l-Fadl, *Ain-i-Akbari*, quoted in A. Sen, 'East and West: The Reach of Reason', in T. Bentley and D.S. Jones (eds), *The Moral Universe* (London: Demos, 2001), p. 13.
40. H. Didier, *Fantòmes d'Islam et de Chine*, pp. 222-3; id., 'Muslim Heterodoxy', pp. 899-900.
41. G.M. Toscano, *Alla scoperta del Tibet* (Bologne: EMI, 1977), p. 43. For Matthew Ricci's letter, see J.J. Wicki (ed.), *Documenta Indica*, vol. XII (Rome: Institutum Historicum Societatis Iesu, 1972), pp. 471-7.
42. K.S. Mathew, 'Akbar and the Europeans', p. 126.
43. E.R. Hambye, 'The First Jesuit Mission to Emperor Akbar', in C.W. Troll (ed.), *Islam in India: Studies and Commentaries*, vol. I (New Delhi: Vikas Publishing House, 1982), p. 6.
44. A. Mariotti, 'La prima missione', p. 76.
45. E. Fasana, 'Introduzione', in E. Fasana and G. Sorge (eds), *India tra Oriente e Occidente*, p. 4.
46. K.S. Mathew, 'Akbar and the Europeans', p. 126.
47. G. Tucci, *Italia e Oriente* (Rome: ISAIO, 2005), p. 61.
48. G. Palumbo, 'La verità disputata', p. 72.
49. Ibid., p. 73.
50. Ibid.
51. Ibid., pp. 73-4.
52. H. Didier, *Fantòmes d'Islam et de Chine,* p. 233.
53. M. Dousse, *Maria la musulmana. Importanza e significato della madre del Messia nel Corano* (Rome: Arkeios, 2006), p. 23.
54. A. Campisi, *Lessico della teologia islamica* (Soveria Mannelli [CZ]: Rubbettino, 2002), p. 15.
55. H. Didier, *Fantomes d'Islam et de Chine*, p. 232.
56. The doctrine of the Christians who lived in Arabia was, however, Semitic, Nestorian or Monophysite.

57. Ibid., pp. 232-4.
58. A. Eraly, *Emperors of the Peacock Throne*, p. 208.
59. A. Ventura, 'Confessioni scismatiche, eterodosse e nuove religioni', in G. Filoramo (ed.), *Islam* (Bari: Laterza, 2012), p. 395.
60. F.C.K.A. von Noer, *The Emperor Akbar: A Contribution Towards the History of India in the 16th Century*, vol. I (Calcutta: Thacker, Spink & Company, 1890), p. 346.
61. For an in-depth exploration of this topic, see Manimugdha S. Sharma's *Allahu Akbar: Understanding the Great Mughal in Today's India* (New Delhi: Bloomsbury, 2019). This book examines the Great Mughal's reign, focusing on his religious and political strategies as well as his spiritual journey. Sharma portrays him as a visionary leader who sought to unify a diverse empire through inclusive governance. The work also addresses misinterpretations of his legacy, highlighting profound spirituality and a commitment to universal peace (*Sulh-i-Kul*). It ultimately offers a fresh perspective on his enlightened leadership and tolerance, with lessons relevant to modern society. See also Elisabetta Colagrossi's *L'eredità contesa: l'impero di Akbar nel conflitto delle interpretazioni* (in A. Grossato [ed.], Religioni e Imperi, [VIlla Verucchio: Pazzini, 2024]), which delves into the interplay between political and religious dimensions of Akbar's reign, underscoring the historical debates surrounding his legacy and the contemporary reinterpretations of his policies and figure.

4

The Third Jesuit Mission at Akbar's Court

REQUEST FOR NEW MISSIONARIES

Akbar was eager and never failed to welcome to his court the most renowned men of letters and artists not only at home but also abroad. He constantly demonstrated his particular sensitivity to philosophical and religious themes, recognizing the enormous value of the European tradition that he knew was steeped in Christian culture, of which the closest and most worthy representatives, as he now knew, could only be the Jesuits. Therefore, the sovereign wanted once again to allow himself the gratifying satisfaction of counting in his entourage some exponents of Western philosophical and theological knowledge, whose expertize would also be related to the activities of the *Maktab Khana*. We repeat that the emperor intended to elaborate a religious reform to allow Islam, once the conservative tendencies had died down, to integrate with Indo-Iranian culture. The emperor, in fact, still needed elaborate arguments against the rigid Sunnite traditionalism, which the group of missionaries, in some way spokesmen for the anti-Islamic Christian polemic, was also able to provide.

The sudden interruption of the second mission (1591) had greatly irritated the Great Mughal; a situation that could certainly cause embarrassment to the Viceroy of the *Estado da Índia*, who understood the usefulness of good relations with his powerful neighbour. In Rome the head of the Society of Jesus could not justify the hasty return to Goa of the fathers, who had precluded any possibility of success for the mission, while for King Philip II of Spain all this could contribute to slow down diplomatic relations with the Mughal government.[1]

In 1594 new hopes were raised when other emissaries of the great Indian sovereign, again accompanied by the indefatigable Armenian interpreter Domingo Pires, arrived in Goa, presenting petitions to the Viceroy Dom Matias de Albuquerque[2] (1547-1609) and to the Jesuit Provincial, Francisco Cabral (1529-1609), in which Akbar requested for the third time that theologians be sent to his court. While it was the Viceroy who had the most serious fears at the time of the Mughal embassy in 1579, it was the Father Provincial who could not see the point of undertaking another mission, which the Goa authorities considered to be of great interest from a political point of view.[3]

After several consultations it was decided to organize a new mission: the Viceroy showed his approval and so did Philip II and the Superior General of the Society of Jesus, Claudio Acquaviva, who suggested to Francisco Cabral to maintain the mission even if the Great Mughal had not expressed his intention to convert to Christianity. In fact, the fathers could still provide an answer to the need to ensure the pastoral care of the different Christian communities.[4] For several decades, many Europeans, especially Portuguese, had settled in the most important Mughal cities, dedicating themselves successfully to artisan and mercantile activities. A number of mercenary adventurers who had freed themselves from the control of the authorities in Goa had also flocked to Akbar's army.[5] Furthermore, in Mughal India there were some Eastern Christians such as Greeks, Syriacs, Chaldeans, Nestorians, but especially Armenians, who constituted the largest group and were also present in the major cities of the empire, such as Agra, Lahore, Patna and Varanasi. Most of them were happily engaged in commerce and quite a few were even landowners, often holding, though not belonging to the aristocracy, influential positions in society. Although the vast majority of these Christians were not Catholics, many of them asked for and were admitted into the communities founded by the Jesuits and were able to participate in the various liturgical celebrations, especially the Eucharist.[6]

MISSIONARY PERSONNEL

As the Jesuit scholar Ángel Santos Hernandes says, 'the choice of the mission superior was an extremely important question both from a religious and a political point of view.'[7] It was, in fact, a delicate task that required not only pastoral skills in the field of evangelization as well as a solid theological and spiritual formation, but also a certain ability to maintain contacts with a court, acting in some way as a representative of the Lusitanian government in Goa, then under the Spanish crown. The Navarrine Jerome Xavier, at that time provost of the Professed House of Goa, was then appointed, to whom were entrusted as companions the Portuguese Manoel Pinheiro (1556-1619) and, as interpreter of Persian, Bento de Góis (1562-1607).[8]

Jerome Xavier

The proper name of the mission's superior was Jerónimo de Ezpeleta y Goni. He therefore belonged to the noble Navarrese family of the same name, which was related to the house of Jasso-Xavier, his maternal grandmother, Ana de Jasso, being the sister of Saint Francis Xavier (1506-52), the Apostle to the Indies, co-founder of the Society of Jesus and a close friend and collaborator of Saint Ignatius of Loyola.[9] Jerome was born in 1549 in the castle of his father, Miguel de Ezpeleta, in Beire, near Olite in the Spanish province of Navarre. He entered the Society of Jesus on 7 May 1568 at the age of nineteen, immediately adopting the surname of his illustrious relative (Xavier)[10] and finishing his novitiate in Toledo with his profession of vows in 1571. After a scrupulous and in-depth philosophical and theological preparation in Alcala de Henares, he decided to go on a mission to the East Indies. On 8 April 1581 he embarked in Lisbon and reached Goa at the end of September.[11]

In the capital of the *Estado da Índia*, Xavier was appointed Master of Novices, but almost immediately had to give up this post due to illness caused by the long and tiring journey by sea and the difficulties of acclimatization. Slowly recovering from his illness, he was admitted to solemn profession of the four vows[12] on 15 January 1584. He was then transferred to Vasai, near present-day Mumbai, where he was Director of the College, but only for a year due to his health problems. So in 1586 he was appointed Rector of Kochi College, which seemed to offer him a climate better suited to his physical well-being.[13] There he took care of the Indian Christians, known as 'St Thomas' Christians,'[14] who attributed the foundation of their community to the disciple of Jesus. In the past these Christians had established links with the Church of Seleucia-Ctesiphon of the Syriac-Oriental (or Chaldean) rite, which after the Council of Ephesus (431) had not accepted Nestorius' condemnation, causing a schism. As a result, the Christians of St Thomas were accused of Nestorianism by the Portuguese, who imposed on them the Latinization of the rite,[15] against which Xavier opposed, although he recognized their subordination to the Latin bishops.[16] He even wrote to Rome in vain to obtain copies of Holy Scripture in Chaldean.[17]

After this intense experience, he was called back to Goa in 1592 to be appointed Superior of the Professed House and to act as *socius* of the Jesuit Father Provincial.[18] Even though he was a Navarrese, because of his training in Alcala he was accused of being a *castellano fino* by the Portuguese Jesuits, who could not accept to obey a Spaniard.[19] These inconveniences, amplified by the growing discontent of the Portuguese with the union of the two crowns in the person of Philip II, were soon overcome. An unexpected solution presented itself to Xavier: Akbar again wished to host a group of Jesuits at his court.[20] Therefore, when the request was submitted, all the members of the *Congregatio Provincialis* chose the Navarrese father as superior of the mission.[21]

Xavier remained at the Mughal court for almost twenty years under the special protection of the emperors, returning to Goa in 1614 to be chosen as Rector of the College. In the meantime he was appointed by Pope Paul V (1552-1621), Coadjutor Bishop of Cranganore,[22] but died on 27 June 1617 before the bull of appointment reached India.[23]

Manoel Pinheiro

There is little, if any, biographical information about Manoel Pinheiro before his important assignment. We know that he was born in 1552 in Ponta Delgada (Azores) and embarked for India in 1590. As for his mission in the Mughal Empire, he was the first to give care and attention to the Indian population, disinterested in the court, but at the same time managed to get into the good graces of the emperor, over whom he came to exert a certain influence. During Jahangir's reign, he also dealt with political matters on behalf of the Lusitanian government to the detriment of the British. He left Mughal India for good in 1614, hoping to return, but his poor health prevented him from doing so; he died in 1619. It is not known precisely why, but probably because of his courageous attempt to adapt to local customs, he was known among the Jesuits as Mogor.[24]

Bento de Góis

The third member of the missionary group, who would become famous above all for having reached China by a long overland journey, was Brother Bento de Góis, a temporal coadjutor, whose religious vocation was not, therefore, called to the priesthood.[25] He had an almost perfect command of the Persian language and his superiors considered him indispensable for the mission to Akbar's court.[26]

Bento de Góis was probably born in 1562 in Vila Franca do Campo, in the Portuguese city of Sao Miguel, an island in the archipelago of the Azores. We do not know the reason or the exact moment when he embarked as a sailor for India, a profession he soon abandoned for that of a soldier once he arrived on the coast of Malabar.[27] Here he began to lead a dissolute and immoral existence until one day in February 1584, while praying on his knees before a statue of the Virgin in a chapel in Kolachal,[28] he felt a deep desire to change his lifestyle and decided to enter the Society of Jesus.[29] However, as soon as he began his spiritual journey with the novitiate, he learnt from his superiors that, for reasons that are not entirely clear to us, he would never receive priestly ordination and so, furious, he left the college and re-enlisted as a soldier in the Lusitanian militia,[30] only to be immediately sent to Hormuz in the Persian Gulf. At the time, Hormuz was an emirate under the protectorate of the Portuguese, who thus had a valuable foothold in Persia, establishing and maintaining more direct relations with Safavid Iran.[31] Hormuz was a thriving commercial town, but apparently not without licentiousness.[32] It is probable that during his four-year stay there, Bento de Góis learned and refined Persian, proving himself fluent in it. We do not know the circumstances under which he applied for and was readmitted to the Society of Jesus in 1588, but in a short time he regained the confidence of his superiors, proving himself not only worthy of deepening and living Ignatian spirituality, but also suitable, above all because of his linguistic skills, for missionary activity, for which he was chosen in 1594 as interpreter to accompany the Jesuit fathers leaving for the Mughal court.[33]

JOURNEY TO AKBAR'S COURT

On 3 December[34] 1594 the three Jesuits, joined by a Portuguese painter and Domingo Pires, embarked in Goa for Daman and from there crossed the borders of Mughal India into the region of Gujarat.[35] The missionaries arrived in Khambat a few days before Christmas and, having to stay there for about three weeks, prepared to celebrate the feast of Christmas.[36]

> We built a chapel and placed an altar there to celebrate the feast of Christ the Child with great emotion, and the Portuguese, who numbered about a hundred, confessed with great spiritual joy [...]. [The chapel was also frequented] by pagans and Moors. When they entered, they pretended to hear something heavenly, saying with ecstasy and amazement: 'God is here! God is here!'. Many of them knelt down to adore the infant Jesus, kissing his feet with the turbans off his head, and likewise in the image of the Virgin, to whom [...] these people show [...] much reverence, respect, courtesy and devotion. So they came in crowds, as if they were Christians, and with such certainty, they came, like us, to our churches, and the most important men were the first.[37]

During this period Xavier also took the opportunity to take some Persian lessons from a Muslim.[38] Also in Khambat, the mission met Akbar's second son, Shahzada Murad Mirza (1570-99), who on his father's orders was advancing against the armies of the Deccan sultanates at the head of an army of fifty thousand men. With great joy, the prince summoned the Jesuits to him[39] and, as Pinheiro writes, 'did us great honour, asking us various things'.[40] After a long conversation, the fathers took their leave of him, but before they left, Murad expressed the wish to offer them money as well as horses and means of transport, but realizing that they would not accept, he handed everything over to Domingo Pires. He then mounted his horse, eager to conduct and regulate military.[41]

The Jesuits also had to set out again, but a journey of about 700 miles awaited them, through regions which, although under the jurisdiction of the Great Mughal, presented certain difficulties. First of all, the land was mainly desert, sometimes sandy, with sometimes strong winds that created dangerous sandstorms. In addition to these natural threats, the attacks of thieves and marauders, of whom the whole area was infested, were a major threat. For all these reasons, those who had to travel this route used to travel in a caravan, that is, together to provide mutual aid, choosing a commander from among themselves to whom they would entrust the leadership of the group, which usually consisted of no less than two thousand travellers.[42]

Obviously, the fathers also found it more reassuring to move as a group rather than in a small autonomous group, so in Khambat they joined Armenian merchants with whom they proceeded to Ahmedabad. In the vicinity of this city one could admire the mausoleum of Sheikh Ahmad Kattu (d. 1446), a famous Muslim saint and spiritual adviser to Ahmad Shah I[43] (d. 1442).

> The work is entirely made of a beautiful, very refined and glossy marble. The brick was made in the same way and had three courses. In one of them, I counted four hundred and forty columns, all in marble, thirty palms high.[44]

In Ahmedabad, the Jesuits also met many Muslims 'who came from land on the continent and from afar. Seeing them so fearful of the Portuguese, I learned that they all went to Mecca and, not finding a way to get there without a Portuguese licence, they fear.'[45]

On 19 March, the fathers left Ahmedabad to arrive on 24 March, which in 1595 coincided with Good Friday, in the city of

Vadodara,[46] where they stayed for three days to celebrate Easter.[47] Here 'many Christians went to confession in the caravan and we had a lot to do with some Armenians' who 'celebrated Easter with us'.[48] Pinheiro informs us that the Armenians had not yet adopted the Gregorian calendar, so that one of them, 'a stubborn old doctor' refused to celebrate Easter with the Jesuits, because he claimed that the Catholics 'were five weeks wrong and did not recognize the authority of the Roman Church. He celebrated Easter on the last Sunday before the Ascension'.[49]

From here on, the reconstruction of the itinerary is extremely problematic, as the letters of the missionaries do not contain references to cities and towns encountered along the way. It would seem, however, that they crossed the Rajputana desert to finally arrive in Lahore on 5 May. Pinheiro recounts:

> We continued our journey, in which we found many very large cities, but many destroyed and with monuments in ruins, especially mosques, which are neither restored nor built. Most of them are pagan. We suffered a lot during this trip because of the lack of water, and the water we found was salty like that of the sea: if I hadn't tried it, I would never have believed it. There was little food, it was very hot and the journey was very long. On the 5th of May we arrived in Lahore, the capital, where Akbar and his court live.[50]

RELIGIOUS FREEDOM IN MUGHAL INDIA

The Jesuits arrived in Lahore on the night of 5 May 1595, but Akbar nevertheless sent one of his captains to welcome them and to attend carefully to their needs.[51] The following day, the fathers went to greet the emperor, who, in the presence of the whole court and his son Salim, 'received them with much honour and cordiality',[52] embracing them and rejoicing at their arrival.[53] For the moment, the ruler carefully avoided talking about religion in his conversations, convinced that the subject could not be properly discussed until all the fathers had learned Persian.[54] So 'with much affection' he invited them to learn that language 'in order to deal' with them 'without an interpreter in the things of salvation'.[55] The festivities with which the emperor honoured them and the kindness shown to them gave hope and foreshadowed a better outcome than in previous missions.[56]

When evening came, the Great Mughal wanted to assign a residence to the missionaries, so he ordered them to be housed 'in a very good house, where he had already lived, near the river, which is as big as the lake, which is near our windows'.[57] In their residence, the fathers improvised a chapel for ordinary prayers and pious exercises. They hadn't brought many tools from Goa, giving more importance to what was indispensable for the journey. The emperor took care of this lack: the first mission had left some sacred images as a souvenir and Akbar gladly gave them to the missionaries, to whom he also gave rich brocade and silk fabrics to decorate the walls and altars.[58]

The Jesuits were also soon able to establish good relations with Salim, the crown prince, who promised to build a church,[59] which was completed in 1597. One could see the amazement in their eyes at the helpful and caring attitude and the attention shown to their religious needs. However, what might have been even more surprising, especially in an Islamic state, was the full freedom given from the beginning to the missionaries to convert all those who wished to embrace Christianity.

In fact, Akbar in 1593, no doubt inspired by the principle of *Sulh-i-kul*, had promulgated an edict of tolerance that granted religious freedom to all regions of the empire. Bada'uni writes with great indignation that 'if any of the infidels chose to build a church, or a synagogue, or idol temple, or Parsee tower of silence, no one was to hinder him'.[60] The sovereign had officially declared that 'no man should be interfered with on account of his religion, and any one should be allowed to go over to any religion he pleased'[61] whereby he ordered that if someone 'had been made a Muslim against his will, he was to be allowed, if he wished, to go back to the religion of his fathers'.[62] The Sunni *ulama* immediately protested, because they saw in this clamorous imperial measure a loss of Islamic pre-eminence in the political and social life of the country: Islam, the only true religion, could certainly not be put on the same level as other faiths.[63]

Hugues Didier argues that in order to better understand the innovative scope of the Great Mughal's bold initiative, it is necessary to consider the distinction between religious tolerance and religious freedom, two concepts that should not be confused. During the

Middle Ages, Christian kingdoms with Jewish minorities in their domains could generally tolerate their religious practices and, if necessary, allow their members to convert to Christianity, but not the other way around. Similar is the tolerance decreed by Muslim law towards the dhimmis, who are allowed to live in the Islamic state and practise their religion upon payment of the *jizya*,[64] a tax that, according to Abu'l-Fadl, Akbar had already abolished in 1564. The emperor, by sanctioning religious freedom at a legal level, seemed to want to eliminate any residue of religious discrimination, so that the Jesuits could, without suffering terrible consequences, erect churches and administer baptism to Muslims who requested it.[65] Thus, according to Didier, 'Mughal India became a land of freedom, without any comparison with the Iberian Peninsula where the Inquisition raged, with England which persecuted its Catholic subjects, or even with the France of the Edict of Nantes.'[66]

However, the local governors and officials did not always respect the imperial dispositions, as happened in Lahore, during a prolonged absence of the king and his court, during which Father Pinheiro was greatly hindered. He therefore felt compelled to appeal to the Great Mughal to obtain a written measure that, with reference to the provisions of the 1593 edict, would guarantee the missionaries the right to carry out their activities freely without disturbance from anyone. As the imperial firman of 1602 stipulates that:

> no creature may penetrate into the house and the church of Father Pinheiro and in no case mix himself up with his affairs and may not molest and importune him. And if someone should become a Christian of his own free will that nobody may prevent him and that he let him act in conformity with his free will.[67]

IN THE EMPEROR'S ENTOURAGE

Jerome Xavier: A Jesuit courtier to the Mughals

During the first two years of the mission, Jerome Xavier, probably assisted by some scholars chosen by the sovereign, was mainly engaged in the study of the Persian language, while Pinheiro and Góis had begun to organize the religious life of the small resident

Christian community, which was made up of heterogeneous ethnic groups but united in faith in Christ. Xavier, having acquired a specific competence in the field of ecclesiastical administration during his first years of apostolate on Indian soil, was interested in religious matters, which also had political consequences. Thus, unlike his two brothers, who rarely went to the imperial palace, he became a regular visitor to the court and was appreciated for his intellectual qualities.[68] Akbar, for his part, seemed to be increasingly interested in Christian doctrine and publicly showed great reverence for the images of Christ, the Virgin and the Apostles carried by the fathers. He was often present at the liturgical celebrations of the Jesuits which, pending the completion of the construction of the church, were still held in the chapel.[69]

During one of his many meetings with the emperor, Xavier showed some letters from the new Father Provincial, Nuño Rodrigues,[70] and two Japanese-style paintings depicting Jesus Christ and St Ignatius of Loyola respectively. Akbar, who had long felt an extraordinary fascination for the themes of Western art, especially religious art, asked the Jesuit many questions about the two works, showing a certain curiosity and interest in the figure of the founder of the Society of Jesus, whose Spiritual Exercises he also owned, probably given to him by the fathers of the first mission. It seems that the court was so impressed by the narration of St Ignatius' life that it requested a transcription in Persian.[71] On another occasion Xavier again presented a letter from Nuño Rodrigues which was read aloud, first in Portuguese, the language in which it was written, then in Persian. During the reading, the emperor showed clear signs of satisfaction as the Father Provincial expressed the most heartfelt appreciation for the benefits and favours granted to the Fathers and through them to all Christendom.[72]

At the end of the letter, the conversation turned, out of curiosity of the emperor himself, to the conflicts between the Christians and the Turks. Xavier unhesitatingly stated that the Ottoman Empire, instead of honouring Christians, who are called to bring the word of salvation to the world, faithful to this commitment even in the face of death, persecuted them because they refused to adhere to Islam. A courtier with whom the missionary had established good relations, noting with disgust how the Muslims present heard these accusations against the Turks, their co-religionists, invited the incautious Jesuit to restrain himself with prudence in expressions that could arouse the indignation of a predominantly Sunni audience, especially in the absence of the emperor, who could not ensure constant monitoring to safeguard his safety.[73]

Although the regular inter-religious debates that had characterized the *Ibadat Khana* at the time of the first mission were no longer in vogue, Xavier, once he had acquired a fair degree of confidence in the use of the Persian language, began to participate in some theological disputes, remembering, however, the advice of his courtier friend on the need to tread carefully so as not to offend the extreme susceptibility of quite a few orthodox Sunnis. Like the meetings that were organized at Fatehpur Sikri, these meetings were always the occasion for endless and unresolved discussions on the most disparate topics and sometimes the emperor even seemed to feel a certain amusement at witnessing these uninterrupted diatribes. Often it was the emperor himself who fomented them, like the one on the question of polygamy and, therefore, of the maximum number of wives allowed, which was already difficult to agree on the different interpretations that exist within the variegated world of Islam. In any case, Akbar asked Xavier, perhaps knowing the answer in advance, what the Christians' position was on the matter. The Jesuit's intervention, from a Muslim point of view, could only be perplexing, since the Church only recognizes monogamous and indissoluble marriage. The king also expressed astonishment at the rigid constraints and limitations to which Christians would be subjected.[74]

The Navarrese missionary practically led the life of a courtier, a condition that allowed him to meet the king frequently and hold conversations with him. This possibility was certainly offered by his recent progress in the study of Persian, but he still needed the mediation of an interpreter. He could, however, even in the wake of comments circulating at the court, begin to form at least semi-definitive impressions of the Great Mughal's religious convictions. For the Jesuit, the emperor's apostasy, albeit tacit, could not but be evident. He could not, however, completely conceal a tendency to adopt positions that seemed to be inspired by what we could define as a sort of theological rationalism, so that in the eyes of the fervent Muslims, as in those of the fathers, he could not but show a presumptuous attitude. At this point the Jesuits also had to reckon with the possibility of yet another disappointment, to which they now seemed accustomed, namely that of not being able to contribute or, if anything, of being witnesses to a new 'Constantinian shift', which would have involved the accession to Christianity of the Great Mughal, perhaps the most powerful Muslim ruler of the time: a real triumph for the Church. This great hope, in fact, tended to fade for the moment, but in a short time the fathers showed their renewed satisfaction in noticing, according to their intuitions, how now, unlike his father, it was the hereditary prince Salim who showed a particularly favourable attitude towards the Christian religion, for which he was soon pointed out as the potential 'Indian Constantine'.

The fact that Akbar was not inclined to embrace Christianity obviously did not cause the Jesuits to close their doors to him. The Jesuits, on the other hand, could not but appreciate his constant cordial and caring behaviour. The sovereign for his part continued to favour the activities of the fathers, allowing them to open a school especially for the children of the Mughal aristocracy. It seems that two of their pupils wished to become Christians, one of whom later even asked to be admitted to holy orders.[75]

Journey to Kashmir

On Easter Day 1597 a great fire struck the imperial residence in Lahore, a misfortune that the Jesuits attributed to the anger of Heaven at the emperor's irreligious presumption. In order to allow the reconstruction of the palace, during the summer Akbar left for Kashmir, taking with him father Xavier and brother Góis, staying in the region from 15 May to 13 November, while Pinheiro had to stay in the capital to take care of the Christians and wait for the completion of the building work on the church.[76] In a letter, Xavier tells us about the difficulties of the journey:

> How much trouble we had in getting through those mountains, which are much bigger than those of our Pyrenees! And, when we had passed one, there was another still worse. For eight or ten days we went from mountain

to mountain, from snow to snow, and under great cold, though it was the end of May. When we arrived at the city and settled down, at once on the third or fourth day both of us, of the Company, fell ill with fever, which lasted us more than two months, and I thought I should become consumptive. For, after I got cured and went about and ate well, I suffered continually night and day from a low fever, which gave me not a little pain and much anxiety; but, as I recovered my strength, it went away, and now I am already out of convalescence, although I enjoy the privileges of it. And the country is specially good for convalescent people: for it is very fresh as to climate, rivers, fountains, surroundings and fields.[77]

The fathers were immediately amazed by the natural and landscape beauty that presented itself to their eyes, but they would soon also be faced with a severe famine that took place in the valley: mothers left their children to die on the roads, while the Jesuits gathered them up and baptized them.[78]

We know that during these years Xavier had devoted himself to the study of Persian, his main occupation since his arrival in Mughal India. In spite of his progress, the difficulties grew, especially because very often, during religious discussions, the Muslims interspersed a multitude of Arabic words in order to put him in difficulty. The Jesuit had accompanied the emperor, also because he hoped to be able to talk privately with him without the help of interpreters, in order to know directly his real intentions towards the mission. But as we have seen, as soon as he arrived in Kashmir he fell ill for two months and after his recovery, it was the sovereign's turn, upsetting the father's plans.[79]

After six months in Kashmir, it was finally decided to return to Lahore. Before leaving, Xavier approached the emperor and asked permission to march in front of the royal party. Many Hindus, who had become attached to their fathers, went to greet them warmly. The inclemency and hardships of the outward journey were repeated on the return: hunger, cold, mountainous roads. The sovereign travelled separately with his retinue, often engaged in hunting activities. On 13 November, Xavier arrived in Lahore and could not help but be delighted to see the construction of the church, which Pinheiro had already inaugurated on 7 September, completed.[80]

The military campaign in the Deccan

A few days later, the emperor also returned to Lahore. He could not conceal his concern about the fate of the war that his army, led by his sons Sultan Murad Mirza and Daniyal (1572-1604), was waging in the Deccan. Although Akbar had now conquered a vast empire stretching across the northern part of the Indian subcontinent from what is now Afghanistan to the Bay of Bengal, he could no longer restrain his eager desire to further expand his domains and so pursued a policy of strong expansion at the expense of the neighbouring sultanates of the Deccan.[81] However, the reason why he wanted to seize this region was above all to secure further footholds for an eventual attack against the Portuguese.[82] Therefore, the Great Mughal's desire to have Jesuits in his entourage could also have been a clever move to obtain information about the military organization of these European settlers.[83] But at the same time, he did not trust his guests, so he avoided talking about his plans in front of them, because he did not rule out the idea that they might have the double role of political agents of Portugal.[84] It seems, in fact, that already in the West, rumours had been circulating for some time about his aims of expansion towards the areas of Lusitanian influence, as we can read in the lines of the Jesuit chronicler Pierre du Jarric, who based himself on the reports that his brethren sent from the various mission fields:

> this powerful monarch desire to make himself master of Goa and the Portuguese possessions in India, with the regions adjacent thereto, that he constantly referred to the subject when conversing with his friends. On one occasion, while speaking of these things to the nobles assembled in his palace, he told them with bold assurance that, having conquered the kingdom of Decan, he would have little difficulty in overcoming Idalcan,[85] after which he would soon have Goa, and all the Portuguese possessions in those parts.[86]

The power of the Lusitanian navy's fleet was celebrated throughout most of the Orient, in spite of the almost total maritime inefficiency of the Mughals, so the ruler concluded that the only way to defeat these Europeans was to avoid fighting at sea and face them on land. Consequently, in order to attack Goa, it was necessary to create several military outposts in the Deccan and win the alliance of the kingdoms of this territory. The emperor seemed to be fully convinced that his powerful and invincible army, which could not be resisted for long, would not only meet no resistance on the march, but would also gain the support of the military forces of the sultanates.[87]

However, Akbar first resorted to diplomacy, sending embassies to every sovereign in 1591 to peacefully request submission to his empire. On that occasion, the Sultan of Khandesh offered his daughter in marriage to Prince Salim, and those of Bijapur and Golconda gifts, but they rejected the emperor's request. Burhan Nizam Shah II (d. 1595), Lord of Ahmednagar, even treated the emissaries of the Great Mughal rudely,[88] so that in 1595 he ordered his sons Murad and Daniyal to launch an attack on Ahmednagar with the support of the Khandesh militia. But the princes, who perhaps unlike their father were not very keen on warlike adventures, preferred, in the face of stubborn resistance, to deal with Chand Bibi (1550-96), regent after the death of the sultan, who ceded Berar to the Mughal Empire.[89] The heroine was assassinated in 1596 and the Ahmednagar Sultanate was in the grip of total anarchy, so Akbar took the opportunity to resume hostilities.[90] In the meantime, however, the Khandesh broke the alliance and his son Murad died as a result of his drinking excesses.[91] The emperor, followed by Xavier and Góis, then decided to transfer the capital to Agra and remained there until 1599, before taking over the military campaign in the Deccan himself.[92]

During this period, the Navarrese Jesuit obtained permission for the introduction of new missionaries into Mughal India, but he also had to inform the monarch that his superiors demanded to know his real intentions towards the mission. Xavier realized that little attention had been paid to them lately by the monarch. The monarch replied that the Deccan War was taking up all his time and energy, but he also pointed out that he had already done a lot for Christianity, as the Jesuits could preach freely in his empire, something unthinkable under the previous rulers.[93]

On the 29 September 1599, the emperor left Agra and a few months later, with his powerful army, he reached Burhanpur, the capital of Khandesh, from where the sultan had fled to take refuge in the fortress of Asirgarh, where he felt most secure, leaving his capital occupied by Mughal troops.[94] Then at the beginning of 1600, Akbar sent Daniyal again, accompanied by General Abdul Rahim Khan-i-Khana[95] (1556-1626) against the city of Ahmednagar, which eventually capitulated.[96] The Great Mughal meanwhile established his headquarters in Burhanpur and from there led the siege of Asigarh,[97] which, contrary to expectations, was not at all easy and took a lot of time for bloody fighting.

Xavier and Góis remained in Burhanpur throughout the conflict, looking after the Christians living in the region. Their long wait was alleviated by the unexpected visit of another missionary, Father Francis Corsi,[98] who arrived in Burhanpur on the feast of the Holy Trinity,[99] destined to Lahore to help Pinheiro in the management of the small but now important and lively Christian community. In order to continue with his destination, through Xavier he managed to obtain from the Great Mughal the necessary safe-conducts to travel freely within his domains. During the time Corsi remained in Burhanpur, he helped his confreres to take care of some Portuguese faithful who were seeking advice and spiritual assistance. The Provincial through the new missionary had sent Xavier an image of Our Lady, which was placed in the chapel, where many Hindus, but especially Muslims, came to admire it. Many of them entered barefoot as in their mosques and when they left, they took a few steps back without their backs to the image, as a sign of deep respect.[100]

Akbar, frustrated by this endless siege and in need of artillery, called Xavier and Góis, begging them to write to Chaul's[101] Portuguese, asking them for guns and ammunition, now indispensable for launching new attacks against the Asigarh. They refused, however, justifying that such an action would be contrary to Christian ethics. Rather, it would seem that the fathers, in addition to knowing the true objectives and intentions of the monarch, as has just been reported, were conditioned by the fact that the Khandesh forces were allied with the Portuguese, who presumably had a few soldiers and officers who had come to support the defence. In any case, the sovereign could only be indignant at the refusal of the Jesuits, to the point of ordering their exile; so, resigned, they prepared to return to Goa, but a courtier dissuaded them from leaving, assuring them that the emperor's anger would not last long. Nevertheless, for some time they had to stay away from his presence.[102]

As if this were not enough, Akbar was informed of a rebellion by his eldest son Salim, who had even proclaimed himself king in Allahabad. Only a timely intervention would have prevented the situation from worsening. It was therefore necessary to find a rapid solution to the conflict and this was possible by bribing the soldiers, probably mercenaries, assigned to defend the fortress.[103] After the capture of Asigarh, the Great Mughal, increasingly worried by Salim's attitude, rushed to Agra, where, however, the alarm seemed to have abated.[104] The emperor, therefore, in order to make up for his son's indiscipline, was forced to interrupt the military campaign, contenting himself with the acquisition of three new provinces for his empire (Khandesh, Berar and Ahmednagar),[105] but renouncing, perhaps forever, his anti-Lusitanian aims.

Before leaving the Deccan, Akbar, in fact, perhaps having to take a step back to restore good relations with the Portuguese, had sent an embassy to Goa led by the Persian Sultan Hamid, previously governor of Gujarat, ordering Góis to accompany him. Arriving in the city at the end of May 1601, the Jesuit immediately retired to his confreres, while the ambassador was received with all honours, even visiting the Jesuit College, to deliver rich gifts from the Great Mughal. Sultan Hamid handed over an imperial petition proposing a political alliance and requesting the sending of skilled craftsmen as well as customs facilities for the purchase of precious stones and other valuable objects. While in Goa, Góis received orders to undertake a journey to the legendary Cathay, which made his name famous. Accompanied by another Jesuit, the Portuguese Antonio Machado[106] (1561-1627), assigned to the Mughal mission, he left Goa in the spring of 1602 and reached Agra in the summer.[107]

During the Deccan campaign, as we know, Pinheiro was left alone in Lahore, turning his attention to the Christian community, which, on the emperor's orders, received every support from the local *subadar* (governor), Khwaja Shams-ud-Din. The Portuguese father also worked successfully to ensure that requests for pardons for those condemned to death were granted. It seems that the missionary's intervention was constantly required: even disputes between high officials were sometimes resolved with his judgement. After the death of Khwaja Shams-ud-Din, Zain Khan Koka was appointed successor, who foiled a series of attempts to discredit the mission. Towards the end of 1600, Pinheiro was happy to finally receive the valuable collaboration of Fr Francis Corsi.[108]

THE LAST YEARS OF AKBAR

The Christian communities of Lahore and Agra

Once the Deccan campaign was partly over, Akbar entrusted the conquered territory to some of his captains and undertook the return journey, arriving in May 1601 in Agra, the new imperial capital.[109] We know that while Xavier remained in the Great Mughal's retinue, Pinheiro and Corsi were busy with the Christian community of Lahore, where soon, despite the imperial signature, which guaranteed them freedom of missionary action, they had to encounter serious interference and obstacles from the new governor, Qulij Khan. Shortly afterwards, the latter was replaced by his son Chin Qulij, who showed a more favourable attitude towards the missionaries, so that they were able to proceed without much worry in their activities.[110]

As we remember, Góis had accompanied a diplomatic mission to the Lusitanian authorities in Goa. There he was instructed to undertake a journey to the mysterious Cathay, in order to verify the existence of an ancient Christian community that had been separated from Rome for centuries due to the expansion of Islam. In 1602, the Jesuit reached Agra with his brother Machado and, having obtained the necessary safe-conducts from Akbar, began a long journey that led him in 1605 near the Great Wall. However, shortly before his death in 1607, he had to bitterly discover that the Cathay and China, already reached by sea by the Portuguese in 1516, were only one country and that there was no trace of ancient Christianity.[111]

In Agra, Xavier, with the help of Antonio Machado, began to turn his attention also to the local Christian community, culturally and ethnically heterogeneous, but now composed of a substantial minority of indigenous converts. As we shall see, in order to attract the attention and curiosity of the population, there were many occasions to make use of the figurative arts and the spectacle of religious ceremonies, in particular solemn and sumptuous processions that wound through the crowded streets of the city. During this period, the fervour also increased due to the display of a copy of the *Madonna del Popolo*[112] in the chapel (pl. 8). Jesuit sources cite thousands of people, Christians, Muslims and Hindus, who came to pay homage to the image. At the emperor's request, the painting was moved to the palace to be admired closely by the courtiers.[113]

Rebellion of Prince Salim

In Mughal India, unlike most kingdoms of the time, especially European ones, in which the crown was generally transmitted by male primogeniture on the death of the sovereign, there was no royal right of succession based on the principle of hereditary monarchy. As a result, there were periodic violent rebellions by princes or fratricidal wars between members of the imperial family themselves. During the last four years of Akbar's reign, the question of succession to the crown arose. Salim, who had remained in Agra during the Deccan War to ensure the safety of the throne, took advantage of his father's absence to rebel and took refuge in the fort at Allahabad. In 1602 he even had Abu'l-Fadl, whom the Great Mughal had sent to persuade him to submit, assassinated. However, the conflict had in the meantime resolved itself: Akbar's other son, Danyal, like Murad, died of his alcoholic excesses in 1604, so that Salim was left as sole successor, unless his son Khusrau was chosen as heir directly. Faced with this possible threat, Salim returned to Agra to perform the act of submission before the sovereign and, after a few days in captivity, was released and treated to all intents and purposes as crown prince.[114]

Akbar's death

Shortly after the reconciliation with his son, Akbar, who had become increasingly exhausted, in October 1605, became seriously ill and died within a short time. Let Xavier himself describe the event of the sovereign's death, the account of which seems to accord with other contemporary testimonies.

The great emperor of India, Akbar, died on October 17th of this year of Our Lord. He died, unhappily, without having had the consolation of entering the bosom of our Holy Religion. He had been suffering from dysentery for some time, but his doctor, believing that he would overcome this ordeal, had given him no medication. The evening after a great elephant battle, he felt very ill and had to stay in bed, not having the strength to appear, as he used to do every day, at the *Jharokha* window to show himself to his people. We were well informed of the progress of the emperor's illness by the intelligences we have in the palace, and on Saturday, October 7, I went with some of our brothers to the fort to see him, hoping that he would be willing to hear the words we had prepared in anticipation of this hour, after we had placed ourselves in the hands of the Lord. But we found him discussing and laughing with his captains with such good humour that we thought it preferable not to speak to him again about the end of his life and decided to wait for another opportunity. So, we left, convinced that he was recovering and that the rumours, as often happens in the case of kings suffering a few days later, that he had suddenly worsened, we returned to the palace, but we could not enter the room where he was lying. Not finding anyone willing to tell him of our arrival, we had to leave. So, we could not see him before he died. According to some, he died as a good Mohammedan, according to others, neither a Hindu nor a sectarian of Mohammed, but in the religion of the Gentiles that he had created. There are persistent rumours that he was poisoned, either by his son Salim—which I refuse to think, as it seems very unlikely—or by mistakenly taking poisoned pills that he had intended to give to one of his enemies at court. But the rumours do not agree on the name of the latter. For my part, it would seem ridiculous to give credence to such nonsense. I have been told that at the last extreme, the sovereign even accused his doctor, Hakîm Alî, of having made him take a harmful remedy. And in fact, the latter would have administered a potion that caused him to become constipated, which would have hastened his end. He immediately became cold.[115]

Shortly before his death, the ruler is said to have solemnly invested his son as his successor. As reported by the chronicler Asad Beg,[116] Akbar 'once more opened his eyes, and signed to them [the amirs around the bed] to invest him [Salim] with the turban and robes which had been prepared for him, and to gird him with his own dagger'.[117] On 3 November 1605, as Salim himself writes, now Emperor Jahangir (Conqueror of the World), 'Having thus seated myself on the throne of my expectations and wishes, I caused also the imperial crown, which my father had caused to be made after the manner of that which was worn by the great kings of Persia'.[118]

END OF THE MUGHAL MISSION

The new Great Mughal immediately thwarted the hopes of the missionaries, since, as a move to legitimize his government, he initially adopted a pro-Sunnite policy. Once he had consolidated his position and prestige, in the religious field, however, he showed himself to be as eclectic and tolerant as Akbar and shared his rationalist theological approach, despite certain mystical and even somewhat esoteric inclinations.[119] In any case, it seems that Jahangir despised the beliefs of Hinduism and Christianity: 'The idea that Christ was the son of god seemed absurd to him, as did the Hindu myths about incarnations.'[120]

During the reigns of the successive emperors, the situation for the Jesuits did not improve, but rather grew more uneasy: both Shah Jahan and Aurangzeb re-established a Sunni theocracy in Mughal India, with the consequent abrogation of the previous measures that had promoted a policy of tolerance under Akbar. In the meantime, the British, who continued to conquer territories and trading bases at the expense of Castilian and Portuguese possessions, soon succeeded in imposing their commercial and maritime hegemony in the whole area. Portugal no longer had sufficient financial means to fulfil its obligations under the *Padroado*, so the Church increased the number of missions organized directly by the *Congregatio de Propaganda Fide*, which entrusted Hindustan to the Carmelites. All these and other factors, together with the subsequent suppression of the Society of Jesus in 1773, determined the end of the Jesuit mission in Mughal India.

NOTES

1. J. Rooney, *The Hesitant Dawn* (Rawalpindi: Christian Study Centre, 1984), p. 42.
2. The Fifteenth Viceroy of Goa from 1591 to 1597.
3. P. du Jarric, *Histoire*, vol. IV, part II (Bordeaux: 1610), p. 463; E. MacLagan, *The Jesuits and the Great Mogul*, p. 50; A.S. Santos Hernandez, *Jeronimo Javier*, p. 108; and J. Rooney, *The Hesitant Dawn*, p. 42.
4. P. du Jarric, *Histoire*, p. 463; J. Rooney, *The Hesitant Dawn*, p. 42; E. MacLagan, *The Jesuits and the Great Mogul*, cit., p. 50; and A.S. Santos Hernandez, *Jeronimo Javier*, cit., p. 108.
5. E. MacLagan, *The Jesuits and the Great Mogul*, p. 268.
6. Ibid., pp. 271-6.
7. A.S. Santos Hernandez, *Jeronimo Javier*, p. 109.
8. P. du Jarric, *Histoire*, pp. 463-4; A.S. Santos Hernandez, *Jeronimo Javier*, p. 109; and E. MacLagan, *The Jesuits and the Great Mogul*, p. 50.
9. A.S. Santos Hernandez, *Jeronimo Javier*, pp. 13-15.
10. A. Camps, *Jerome Xavier S.J. and the Muslims of the Mogul Empire: Controversial Works and Missionary Activity* (Schoneck-Beckenried: Nouvelle Revue de Science Missionnaire, 1957), pp. 2-3.
11. A.S. Santos Hernandez, 'Dos Javieres en la India', *Miscelanea Comillas*, vol. 10, no. 18 (1952), pp. 31-2.
12. Poverty, chastity, obedience and a vow to the Pope about one's availability for the mission.
13. A. Camps, *Jerome Xavier*, p. 3.
14. H. Didier, *Fantomes d'Islam et de Chine*, p. 237.
15. J. Étèvenaux, *Histoire des missions chrétiennes* (Saint-Maurice: Saint-Augustin, 2004), pp. 57-8.
16. H. Didier, 'Jerónimo Javier, un avarro en la India', in V. Maurya and M. Insua (eds), *Actas del I Congreso Ibero-Asiatico de Hispanistas Siglo de Oro e Hispanismo General* (Pamplona: Universidad de Navarra, 2011), p. 148.
17. Id., *Fantomes d'Islam et de Chine*, p. 237.
18. The *socius* replaces the Father Provincial in the event of incapacity, illness or absence.
19. H. Didier, 'Jerónimo Javier', p. 148; and id., *Fantomes d'Islam et de Chine*, p. 238.
20. Ibid.

21. A. Camps, *Jerome Xavier*, pp. 3-4.
22. Currently, Kodungallur is an Indian town in the district of Thrissur, in the federal state of Kerala.
23. E. MacLagan, *The Jesuits and the Great Mogul*, p. 51. For further biographical information, please refer to the following texts already cited: A.S. Santos Hernandez, *Jeronimo Javier*; and A. Camps, *Jerome Xavier*.
24. A.S. Santos Hernandez, *Jeronimo Javier*, p. 109; and E. MacLagan, *The Jesuits and the Great Mogul*, p. 51.
25. H. Didier, *Fantomes d'Islam et de Chine*, p. 16.
26. Ibid., p. 18. We know that the ruler aimed to make Persian not only the *only administrative language* allowed in Mughal India, but also the *only language of the people*, a vehicle for communication between the different ethnic groups. Persian had for some time—under the influence of Safavid Iran—also the language of the culture of Asian Islam, and therefore an international language, spoken from the Ottoman Empire as far as the western borders of China (ibid.).
27. Ibid.; id., 'Ormuz', pp. 172-3.
28. Currently, it is an Indian town in the Kanyakumari district of the federal state of Tamil Nadu.
29. H. Didier, *Fantomes d'Islam et de Chine*, p. 16.
30. V. Cronin, *The Wise Man from the West: Matteo Ricci and His Mission to China* (London: Fount Paperbacks, 1984), p. 227.
31. H. Didier, *Fantomes d'Islam et de Chine*, pp. 16-17. The Safavid Empire had adopted Shi'a Islam as its state religion, a further cause of friction with the Ottoman Turks, staunch defenders of Sunnism (ibid.).
32. Ibid.
33. Ibid., pp. 17-18; id., 'Ormuz', p. 173.
34. The date on which St Francis Xavier died and since 1623 a liturgical feast is celebrated in his honour, which is considered the patron saint of missions.
35. G. Peruschi, *Informatione*, p. 40.
36. I. de Guzman, *Historia de las missiones que han hecho los religiosos de la Compunta de Iesus para predicar el Sancto Evangelio en la India Orientai, y en los Reynos de la China y Iapon* (Alcala: Viuda de Juan Gracián, 1601), vol. III, pp. 257-8; and P. du Jarric, *Histoire*, pp. 464-5.
37. A letter from Manoel Pinheiro, quoted in G. Peruschi, *Informatione*, pp. 41-2.
38. A. Camps, *Jerome Xavier*, p. 181.

39. P. du Jarric, *Histoire*, p. 465.
40. A letter from Manoel Pinheiro to João Alvarez of 3 September 1595, quoted in G. Peruschi, *Informatione*, p. 62.
41. P. du Jarric, *Histoire*, pp. 465-6.
42. Ibid., pp. 467-8; and I. de Guzman, *Historia*, p. 260.
43. He was the Sultan of Gujarat from 1411 until his death.
44. A letter from Manoel Pinheiro to João Alvarez, quoted in G. Peruschi, *Informatione,* p. 63.
45. Ibid.
46. An Indian city located in the federal state of Gujarat. It is about 60 miles from Ahmedabad.
47. A letter from Manoel Pinheiro to João Alvarez of 3 September 1595, quoted in G. Peruschi, *Informatione*, p. 64.
48. Ibid.
49. Ibid.
50. Ibid., pp. 64-5.
51. A.S. Santos Hernandez, *Jeronimo Javier,* p. 114.
52. A letter from Jerome Xavier to Claudio Acquaviva, Lahore, 20 August 1595, quoted in J. Wicki (ed.), *Documenta Indica*, vol. XVII, p. 69.
53. A letter from Manoel Pinheiro to João Alvarez, Lahore, 3 September 1595, quoted in G. Peruschi, *Informatione*, p, 65.
54. E. MacLagan, *The Jesuits and the Great Mogul*, p. 54.
55. A letter from Jerome Xavier to Claudio Acquaviva, Lahore, 20 August 1595, quoted in J. Wicki (ed.), *Documenta Indica*, vol. XVII, p. 69.
56. E. MacLagan, *The Jesuits and the Great Mogul*, p. 54.
57. A letter from Manoel Pinheiro to João Alvarez, Lahore, 3 September 1595, quoted in G. Peruschi, *Informatione*, p. 65.
58. A.S. Santos Hernandez, *Jeronimo Javier,* p. 115.
59. Ibid.
60. Bada'uni, *Muntakhab al-Tawarikh*, quoted in A. Eraly, *The Last Spring: The Lives and Times of the Great Mughals* (New Delhi: Viking, 1997), p. 220.
61. Ibid., p. 211.
62. Ibid., p. 220.
63. H. Didier, *Fantòmes d'Islam et de Chine,* p. 239.
64. Ibid. Instituted by the second Islamic caliph, 'Omar ibn al-Khattab (581-644), the *jizya* was initially imposed only on Jews, Christians and, later, Zoroastrians, who were granted the status of *dhimmi* (protected), as *Ahl-al-Kitab*' (People of the Book) and, therefore, tolerated and respected, as the Koran itself would invite them to do (Sura 2, 62; 9, 29); whereas the *kafir* (unbelievers) were not even given the right

to exist. The *jizya*, made compulsory for the first time in India by Muhammad bin Qasim (695-715), who, not wanting to commit genocide, extended the status of *dhimmi* to Hindus and Buddhists as well (ibid., pp. 213-14, 239, 322; S.A.A. Rizvi, 'Dimensions of Sulh-i Kul', pp. 4-5; I. Pellicani, *I Rajput: Storia, leggende e tradizioni dei Samurai dell'India* [Roma: Newton Compton, 1994], p. 43).

65. H. Didier, *Fantomes d'Islam et de Chine,* p. 239.
66. Ibid., pp. 239-40.
67. Firman of Emperor Akbar from 1602, quoted in P. Jackson, 'Christian–Muslim Dialogue in India', *Studia Missionalia* (Rome: Pontificia Università Gregoriana, 1994), vol. XLIII, p. 162.
68. L. Frédéric, *Akbar le Grand Moghol*, p. 314.
69. Ibid.
70. He was the Father Provincial of Goa from 1597 to 1602.
71. A.S. Santos Hernandez, *Jeronimo Javier,* p. 122. It is probable that Xavier wrote some books on the lives of the saints, which may have contained a biography of St Ignatius, but these have not come down to us.
72. Ibid., p. 122.
73. Ibid., p. 123.
74. Ibid.
75. Ibid.
76. Ibid., pp. 129-30; and E. MacLagan, *The Jesuits and the Great Mogul*, p. 55.
77. A letter from Jerome Xavier to Thomas de Iturén, Srinagar, 1 September 1597, quoted in *Journal and Proceedings of the Asiatic Society of Bengal* (Calcutta: Asiatic Society of Bengal, 1923), vol. XXIII, p. 116.
78. E. MacLagan, *The Jesuits and the Great Mogul*, p. 55.
79. A.S. Santos Hernandez, *Jeronimo Javier,* pp. 131-3.
80. Ibid., pp. 136-7.
81. L. Frédéric, *L'Inde de l'Islàm* (Paris: Arthaud, 1989), p. 189. At that time in the Deccan, a region located in the central part of the Indian peninsula, there were five Muslim sultanates: the *Khandesh*, under the Farruqi dynasty, the only ones to pay tribute to the Mughals; the *Ahmednagar*, under the Nizam; the *Bijapur*, under the Adil Shahi; the *Golconda*, under the Qutb; and the *Berar*, under the Imad. This last sultanate was, however, annexed in 1574 by the *Ahmednagar* (F. Richards, *The Mughal Empire*, p. 53; and R.S. Chaurasia, *History of Medieval India: From 1000 A.D. to 1707 A.D.* [New Delhi: Atlantic, 2002], p. 103).
82. L. Frédéric, *L'Inde de l'Islàm*, p. 189.

83. Ibid.
84. Id., *Akbar le Grand Moghol*, cit., p. 320.
85. Adil Khan, *hakim* (ruler, governor) of Bijapur.
86. P. du Jarric, *Akbar and the Jesuits: An Account of the Jesuit Missions to the Court of Akbar* (London: Harper & Brothers, 1926), p. 55.
87. Id., *Histoire*, vol. V, part III, p. 39.
88. J.F. Richards, *The Mughal Empire*, pp. 53-4.
89. Ibid., p. 54; Frédéric, *L'Inde de l'Islàm*, p. 191.
90. Ibid.
91. J.F. Richards, *The Mughal Empire*, cit., p. 54.
92. E. MacLagan, *The Jesuits and the Great Mogul*, p. 57.
93. Ibid.
94. J.F. Richards, *The Mughal Empire*, p. 54; and L. Frédéric, *Akbar le Grand Moghol*, pp. 321-4.
95. He is the son of Bairam Khan (*c.* 1513-61), the regent of the Mughal Empire during Akbar's childhood.
96. L. Frédéric, *L'Inde de l'Islàm*, p. 191.
97. Id., *Akbar le Grand Moghol*, pp. 324-5.
98. He was born in Pistoia in 1568, entered the Society of Jesus in 1585 and, after his religious studies, left for Goa in 1599. He died on 1 August 1635, during the reign of Shah Jahan. For further biographical information, see R.M. Cimino, 'Un missionario italiano alla corte dei "Mogor": il Padre Francesco Corsi', E. Fasana and G. Sorge (eds), *Civiltà indiana ed impatto europeo nei secoli XVI-XVIII: L'apporto dei viaggiatori e missionari italiani* (Milan: Jaca Book, 1987), pp. 201-22.
99. The feast of the Holy Trinity in 1600 fell on 28 May.
100. A.S. Santos Hernandez, *Jeronimo Javier*, pp. 151-3.
101. A port situated not very far from Burhanpur; today practically in ruins. It is located in the present Raigad district of the federal state of Maharashtra.
102. A.S. Santos Hernandez, *Jeronimo Javier*, p. 155; and E. MacLagan, *The Jesuits and the Great Mogul*, p. 58.
103. L. Frédéric, *L'Inde de l'Islàm*, p. 191.
104. Ibid.
105. M. Gaborieau, 'Akbar et la construction de l'empire (1556-1605)', p. 112.
106. Information about his life and his missionary activity is scarce, almost non-existent.
107. A.S. Santos Hernandez, *Jeronimo Javier*, pp. 156-9; and E. MacLagan, *The Jesuits and the Great Mogul*, pp. 58-9.

108. Ibid., pp. 56-7.
109. A.S. Santos Hernandez, *Jeronimo Javier*, p. 162.
110. E. MacLagan, *The Jesuits and the Great Mogul*, pp. 59-61; and R.M. Cimino, 'Un missionario italiano alla corte dei "Mogor"', pp. 208-9.
111. For a more detailed account of Brother Góis' long and arduous journey to the mythical Cathay, the following extensive bibliography can be consulted: H. Didier, *Fantòmes d'Islam et de Chine*, pp. 7-206; 251-82; id., 'Le non publié et l'impubliable: le cas des Jésuites missionaries en terre d'Islam, XVIe-XVIIIe siècles', *Transversalités: Revue de l'Institut catholique de Paris* (July-September 2007), pp. 15-25; P. Lécrivain, '"Cherchant le Cathay, il trouva le Ciel...": Bento de Góis S-J. en Asie Centrale (1602-1607)', *Transversalités* (April-June 2012), pp. 13-27; M. Ricci, *Della entrata della Compagnia di Giesù e Christianità nella Cina* (Macerata: Quodlibet, 2000), pp. 511-35; G.M. Toscano, *Alla scoperta del Tibet*, pp. 44-6; C. Wessel, *Early Jesuit Travellers in Central Asia* (Delhi: Low Price Publications, 1999), pp. 1-41; V. Cronin, *The Wise Man from the West*, pp. 226-45; G. Bishop, *In Search of Cathay: The Travels of Bento de Goes, S.J. (1562-1607)* (Anand: Gujarat Sahitya Prakash, 1998).
112. The original is a twelfth to thirteenth century Byzantine panel, traditionally attributed to St Luke, which is on the high altar of the Church of Santa Maria del Popolo in Rome.
113. A.S. Santos Hernandez, *Jeronimo Javier*, pp. 188-9.
114. M. Gaborieau, 'Akbar et la construction de l'empire (1556-1605)', p. 112.
115. A letter from Jerome Xavier to the Provincial Father of Goa, Manoel de Veiga, Agra, in October 1605, quoted in L. Frédéric, *Le tigre et la rose: Une passion à la cour des Grands Moghols* (Paris: Robert Laffont, 1984), pp. 133-4.
116. He was a disciple and in the service of Abu'l-Fadl until the latter's death. He remained at the imperial court until the reign of Shah Jahan. He wrote the *Waqa'i' Asad Beg*, which is interesting for the study of internal Mughal politics (M.L. Gupta, *Sources of Mughal History, 1526 to 1740* [New Delhi: Atlantic, 1989], p. 77).
117. Asad Beg Qazwini, *Waqa'i' Asad Beg*, quoted in A. Early, *Emperors of the Peacock Throne*, p. 228.
118. Jahangir, *Tuzuk-i-Jahangiri*, quoted in ibid., p. 229.
119. Ibid., p. 241.
120. Ibid.

5 Missionary Activities

RESISTANCE TO CONVERSION

The Hindus

Considering the impossibility of an adhesion to Christianity on the part of the emperor and his court as a given, but strong in the religious freedom he had proclaimed, the fathers of the third mission began almost immediately, albeit with a certain caution, to dedicate themselves to the organization and implementation of proselytizing activities oriented towards the conversion of the indigenous population. As we can remember, the majority of the subjects of the Mughal Empire professed Hinduism, a religion that considers the life of every man as predetermined, without any possibility of redemption or affirmation for the less well-off social classes. Therefore, it was above all the pariahs (outcasts) who requested baptism, since initiation into the Christian religion presented itself mainly as an opportunity to escape from a condition of economic and social marginalization.

Even the Muslims, who had been present in India for several centuries, had not made many sincere and profound conversions. In fact, the few Hindus who had voluntarily or forcibly abandoned their religion for that of Muhammad, came mostly from the lower classes and therefore aspired to a higher social position.[1] Generally, for those who belonged to one of the upper castes of Hindu society, it was not convenient, if not risky, to convert to another faith, since abandoning the ancestral religion to embrace another one resulted in social ostracism: apostates became downgraded people and were no longer admitted in the community, even losing any right to inheritance.

Not very edifying, but above all not very profitable for the missionary activity, could be the news coming from the *Estado da Índia* about episodes related to the destruction of temples and the persecution of Hindus by the Portuguese colonists, whom the Jesuits represented in some way.[2]

The Muslims

Attempts to evangelize the Muslim population, for a variety of reasons, have also had little success. As in other missions in Islamic lands, Catholic preachers seem to be resigned to the impossibility of converting Muslims, which at first glance seems to be due to the possible terrible consequences of joining Christianity.[3] Muslim law (*Shari'a*), which is based on both the Koran and the *Hadith*, prescribes capital punishment for the crime of apostasy. Although the Koran limits itself to the condemnation to hell for those who abandon Islam,[4] a *Hadith* of Muhammad says:

> It is not lawful to shed blood of a person professing Islam [...], except in three cases: life for a life, or a married person guilty of adultery or a person who separates from his faith and deserts his community.[5]

In Mughal India, Akbar's policy of religious reform averted the danger of death sentences for apostasy. However, it was still difficult, if not impossible, not to feel the influence of one's family, cultural and religious affiliation. Islamic society always exercised a certain coercion that prevented individuals from converting.[6]

In the eyes of the missionaries, as well as in the collective imagination of the West, the 'fanaticism' of the Muslim was the first cause of hindrance to the mission. He was hardly receptive to the Gospel message. His was the pride of those who presume to belong to the chosen people and to hold the truth in a complete and universal form.[7] In fact, according to a theory that closely resembles

Tertullian's thesis of the *anima naturaliter christiana*, Islam presents itself as *din al-fitra*, that is, as the religion of man's original condition.[8] The Islamic faith shows, therefore, a universal character and is 'considered innate to every man and even subscribed to by the whole of humanity in a mysterious primordial pact made with God even before creation'.[9] God has made a pact (*mithaq*) with mankind, which he periodically reminds men of throughout history through his prophet-legislators.[10] Muhammad would be the last to recall a message that is always fundamentally the same, ever since Adam. History will end with the Final Judgement that will allow us to verify whether this covenant has been respected by every human being.[11]

A famous *Hadith* attributed to the Prophet states that, 'Every man is born a Muslim; his parents make of him a Christian or a Jew.'[12] As we can guess, Judaism and Christianity would be nothing but falsified and later expressions of Islam. The biblical characters themselves, as well as Jesus and the Apostles, could only be Muslim prophets. From this point of view there is no link between Christianity and Judaism, but a direct and necessary filiation of Christianity from Islam is recognized. In other words, for the Muslim, Christianity would be a derivation, or rather a deviation, from Islam, the original and fundamental religion of all humanity.

Being in accordance with human nature, Islam is also the religion of reason, and it is the only religion that allows the attainment of happiness.[13] Therefore, the Muslim believer is the one who allows himself to be guided by his soul, by his intelligence along the path of his own fulfilment as a man, as a creature among creatures.

On the basis of what has just been said, it is clear that the conversion of Muslims was, and still is, something extraordinary in every sense of the term. What made this type of apostolate even more difficult was certainly the impasse caused by centuries of mutual incomprehension, inveterate hatreds and grudges that had never been laid to rest between the two civilizations, the Christian and the Islamic. The missionaries wanted to spread the religion of the *Pranguis*, a derogatory term used by the Muslims to refer to Christians since the Crusades. In the eyes of the Mughal population of Islamic and Hindu faith, the Jesuits personified the power of Lusitania with all its expansionist and hegemonic aims. Although

Portuguese colonization did not contemplate in-depth penetration, the presence of these Europeans on the Indian coast, with the consequent control of maritime traffic, was experienced as an intrusion, as well as constituting a threat to pilgrims going to Mecca. And, to complete the picture, as a further cause of indignation, anger and disgust at the horrors of Portuguese colonialism and its expansionist wars, there would finally be the establishment in 1560 in Goa of the tribunal of the Holy Inquisition, which particularly targeted the Marranos, the converted Jews, and, indeed, the Mouros, the local Muslims.[14] On the basis of the prevailing Islamic conception, which considers religion as directly affecting every political and social field, Christianity could only be considered as the religious side of the colonial enterprise. Christians were assimilated with Europeans, whose behaviour seemed not very 'evangelical' in the eyes of the populations. Muslims could not help but feel annoyed when Catholic preachers tried to convert them, since they already believed in God. Nor could they accept being treated as pagans, they, the champions of the *Tawhid*. Therefore, their reaction towards those who, like the Jesuit fathers, flaunted exclusively religious intentions, could only be one of distrust. It was suspected, in fact, that behind the intentions of the missionaries there was actually a broader project that envisaged the subjugation of Islamic countries to Christian kingdoms, therefore to powers of another religion. The Muslims refused *a priori* to be subjected to a multiform domination that would have effectively combined the economic, social, cultural and, above all, religious spheres.[15]

We do not want to omit to underline that presumably, to make the evangelization of the populations of Mughal India even more difficult, there was also the often hostile attitude of the missionaries towards not only the Muslims but also the Hindus, which obliged them to be on the defensive.[16] It seems that this behaviour shown by the fathers was a consequence of the difficulty in fully understanding, at least initially, the reality that hosted them. In fact, precisely because of the type of apostolate we are dealing with here, the persons concerned often lacked a preliminary and adequate linguistic, cultural and religious formation, which had to be made up with time and experience in the field. However, it is worth remembering that the three missions in Mughal India were always the result of a surprising and unexpected initiative of the Emperor Akbar, so one can imagine how the political and religious authorities of Goa delayed as long as possible in order to be able to organize 'on the spur of the moment' what was requested by the Great Mughal, without having, as a consequence, the necessary time to provide further careful preparation of the already certainly qualified missionary personnel.[17] At this point we are also able to hypothesize the possibility that an initial task assigned to the Jesuits was precisely that of gathering information to study and elaborate some useful strategies for this mission field that was still, in some ways, unripe and therefore difficult.

MISSIONARY METHODS

After an initial period of observation, the fathers began to formulate and experiment with different missionary methods, which took into account the specificity of the environment in which they worked and the double orientation of their mission: towards the court and towards the local population.

It was evident that the acquisition of a certain mastery of the languages spoken in the territory was one of the pre-requisites that could not be ignored for the very existence of the mission. As we know, Jerome Xavier's first task was to study Persian, which would gradually enable him to participate in the court life and have private conversations with the emperor. Once he proved to be fluent in Persian, the Jesuit repeatedly had the opportunity to take part, without the aid of an interpreter, in the lively discussions on the most controversial issues taking place in the palace.

Let us remember that the efforts of the missionaries were not only directed towards maintaining good relations with the emperor and his court, but also towards the complete pastoral care of the Christians residing in Mughal India. It has been mentioned in the earlier chapter that they formed a heterogeneous ethnic-religious group comprising European Catholics, Eastern Christians and Indian converts; therefore, the Jesuits considered it indispensable to appeal to the same faith in Christ as the first element of identity cohesion, irrespective of the different ritual and disciplinary traditions.

Pinheiro and Góis, having made quite a few conversions of 'outcast' Hindus, although one may doubt their sincere adherence to the Gospel, certainly recognized the importance of mastering vernacular languages, but, by analogy with Islamic ritual in which Arabic is the sacred language, they decided to adopt Portuguese as the Christian sacred language. This choice proved to be impractical from the outset, making it necessary, at least for the time being, to resort to translations and explanations of sacred texts, doctrines and Christian rituals in Persian.[18] As time went by, however, there was a growing need to use the languages spoken by the population in preaching, teaching catechism and the liturgy, especially Hindustani, which was the language used by the majority. The transposition of the Christian cult into the local idioms was obviously not a simple and immediate operation, but required a relatively long period that lasted during Jahangir's reign.

In the meantime, the Jesuits relied heavily on the spectacularization of liturgical celebrations, without distorting them, in order to increase their interest and attractiveness. In order to be in tune with the tastes of the Indian public, religious ceremonies were always held with a certain sumptuousness and solemnity.[19] During the important festivals, special attention was paid to the decoration of the churches, their external lighting and the frequent use of fireworks to increase the luminosity.[20] In addition to the solemn and pompous processions, the mysteries, theatrical representations of biblical events, were particularly popular. These were often accompanied and interspersed with explanations and comments by the fathers or catechumens, but often young men dressed in angelic robes held signs with the biblical text written in Persian.[21] It seems that sometimes the Jesuits impersonated the figure of Jesus, as witnessed by some Mughal paintings in which Christ is portrayed in Jesuit garb (pls. 1 and 2); so, we could also suppose that the painters of the imperial atelier, for the depiction of some Gospel scenes, were not directly inspired by the Holy Scripture but by these theatrical representations.[22] Finally, there was no shortage of social entertainment, with jugglers, tightrope walkers, acrobats and jugglers, nor were there any musical performances, either instrumental or vocal.[23] The fathers' celebrations were attended not only by ordinary subjects, but also by a large number of courtiers and even the emperor himself. In fact, both Akbar and Prince Salim regularly provided money, candles, fabrics and decorative images for these events as well and the Christian festivities were soon counted among the main attractions of the Mughal social calendar.[24]

As in other Jesuit missions, the fathers who resided in the Mughal Empire attempted an accommodation of Christianity to the indigenous culture, which implied, in this case, a fusion of Christian elements with Indo-Iranian cultural and religious elements.[25] For example, they adopted the local custom of carrying new converts on elephant backs through the streets and, in particular, the Islamic devotion to the sacred text.[26] The missionaries had carefully observed the profound respect shown by Muslims for the Koran, inimitable in form and content, as God would have it descend (*nazzala*) to men from heaven in the Arabic language.[27] The most eloquent gesture to express this sentiment was to place the book on one's head; a gesture that the Jesuits and their followers imitated, but which they performed with respect to the Bible. Moreover, in solemn processions the Holy Scripture was often exposed to public veneration.[28] As Hugues Didier points out: 'the Indo-Iranian and even, to a certain extent, Islamic inculturation of the mission of the Great Mughal can also be seen in the fact that it was decided that in the churches a curtain would separate the sexes: as in the mosques'.[29]

CHRISTIAN SUBJECTS IN MUGHAL PAINTING

During their stay in Hindustan, the Fathers sent from Goa and Europe copies of paintings and prints with Christian subjects, especially Mary, Jesus, some saints, the Apostles and angels, to be exposed to public veneration or used as models by the Mughal artists. We also know that a Portuguese painter, whose name and life we do not know, had come to the court under the auspices of the Jesuits, in order to make himself available to the ateliers of Akbar and Salim. Xavier writes that the prince immediately ordered the Lusitanian artist to paint 'a copy of a painting of the Madonna that we had with us', since 'he was really furious with that Moor who accompanied us [from Goa to Lahore] for not having brought him any image of the Mother of God'.[30] As I am sure the missionaries were already aware, the emperor had been interested in Christian figurative art since his first mission. Father Pinheiro affirms that since some time ago, the Great Mughal possessed 'some images of Christ our Lord and Our Lady of a certain value, coming from Europe, and preserves them with great decency and respect.'[31]

For several decades a prolific painting workshop had been established in Mughal India, to which the most renowned Persian and Indian artists, both Hindu and Muslim, had flocked. This new school, which already presented itself as an original synthesis of painting styles from different countries of the East, was also able to incorporate the major innovations of European art.[32] Nevertheless, it was the Jesuit missions that contributed to a greater and faster acceleration of the European influence on Mughal painting.[33] The emperor's artists made several copies of works of Christian figurative art, re-adapting elements and motifs.[34]

The use of sacred images as a useful tool for religious instruction

The Jesuits in their missions often resorted to the use of sacred images to facilitate the communication of Christian doctrines, also remedying the inevitable difficulty of quickly mastering the local languages.[35] We know that the fathers of the first Mughal mission, following Akbar's request to bring the Holy Scriptures to the Christians, presented him with the volumes of the famous Polyglot Bible of Antwerp, which contained engravings by well-known artists of the Flemish school, including the Wierx brothers. The idea of offering illustrated books to the Great Mughal might reveal a possible strategy of explaining the sacred text through images.[36] Indeed, the Jesuits attributed to images an immediate capacity for communication, an idea that, together with their ability to imprint themselves in the memory, is found in many post-Tridentine authors.[37] Compared to the word, then, the image appeared to have a greater force of impact, due to the fact that it was intuitive, immediate, synthetic and, above all, universal.[38]

The didactic value of the image, as it captures the visual senses and leads man to the recognition of a higher truth, was one of the main arguments in favour of the use of images proposed by the Council of Trent (1545-63) in opposition to Protestant aniconism. Art historian Emma Devapriam (1933-2005) writes:

> Realizing the importance of religious imagery in religious instruction, the Council approved the use of images but strictly defined their role. As the effectiveness of the images was perceived as being directly dependent upon the realism with which they are imbued, the Council recommended that they should be straightforwardly realistic and that they should represent a particular emotional stimulus to piety [...]. Contrary to the Manneristic portrayal, they were expected to be represented with singular clarity, and ready intelligibility. The Counter-Reformation, a movement inaugurated by Council of Trent, propagated these conceptions of art [...]. The Jesuits, who hoped to strengthen the Church of Rome and establish it as the Universal Order of Christianity became an important instrument of the Counter-Reformation. Although historians have argued that there is no Jesuit style, their contribution towards 'realism' in art cannot ignored.[39]

The Jesuits and the defence of sacred images

The Fathers, having to remain in an Islamic state, could also expect the possibility of an iconoclastic attitude on the part of the Mughal sovereign and the court.[40] As the historian and theologian François Boespflug states, 'Contrary to what one sometimes hears, the Koran contains no formal condemnation of images[41] as such nothing really comparable to the Jewish prohibition in the Decalogue, an imperious and unconditional prohibition.'[42]

A hostile attitude towards painting can only be found in the *Hadith*. In the Koran, the term used to indicate God's creative activity (Bara'a, to create) is synonymous with the term used to designate the work of the artist (Ṣawwara, to shape, to form).[43] So, the painter,

> When he represents a living being, he assumes a blasphemous attitude: he intends to compete with God. The day of Judgement will be worth the punishment he deserves, for God will order him to breathe life into the creatures he has represented, and his impotence will be harshly punished.[44]

Secondly, explicit condemnations to the representation of the divinity are superfluous, because 'the God of Islam is one, absolute, radical and so marked by absence that the prohibition to represent him comes from his conception'.[45]

The intransigent attitude of Islam, which also seemed to be justified by the Decalogue, required not only a solid theological preparation on the part of the Jesuits, but also a certain oratorical and persuasive ability to defend the lawfulness and usefulness of sacred images. As Anthony Montserrat writes, the early mission fathers, using the arguments of post-Tridentine authors, claimed that

> God had only prohibited the making and worship of images of false gods [...]. [In fact, in the Bible] the words 'graven image' and 'idol' denote only the images of demons and false gods; and God, Creator of the universe, forbade both in law and Gospel the worship of such images. Wherefore it is wrong to accuse of idolatry Christians who do reverence to the painted or carven image of God and divine beings.[46]

Jerome Xavier, during a religious debate, pointed out that Christians 'do not venerate the images for what they are, because we are well aware that they are merely paper or canvas with pigments; it is because of those whom they represent'.[47] Finally, according to the Jesuit, it is good to remember the main function of sacred images: to make present the deeds of Christ and the saints.[48]

The Great Mughal's interest in the realistic style

As we have just said, the Jesuits probably expected to find an iconoclastic environment in Mughal India, but Akbar did not obey the stereotypical European image of the Muslim ruler, revealing, on the contrary, a strong attraction for Christian figurative art.[49] The emperor was also particularly interested in the arguments in favour of the use of sacred images. This attitude only gave rise to further false hopes about the possibility of his accession to Christianity. The fathers were also convinced that devotional paintings had the power to arouse not only veneration for what they represented, but also the conversion of the court and the Mughal population. Thus, the sacred images, as we know, were not only presented to the Great Mughal and his entourage, but also displayed in churches or carried in processions; according to Jesuit sources, which mention some miraculous healings, thousands of people flocked to pay their respects.[50]

After a short time, however, the fathers found that their images did not have the desired effect: the emperor and the courtiers did not adhere to Christianity, nor did mass conversions of the population follow. Nevertheless, their paintings were always the object of great interest on the part of the ruler. Thus, scholars have often wondered why the Great Mughal and his court felt a particular attraction for European devotional art. According to Abu'l-Fadl 'His Majesty, from his earliest youth, has shewn a great predilection for this art, and gives it every encouragement.'[51] Moreover, he did not hide a certain preference for realistic images,[52] so his artists were inevitably pushed in this direction. 'Contact with European art increased the sense of observation in the Mughal painter, resulting in a heightened realism in Mughal painting.'[53] What fascinated the sovereign's artists about Western paintings were the approach to corporality, the rendering of drapery, as well as the spatial depth that was achieved by resorting to central perspective with the consequent reduction in perspective of the figures.[54] Therefore, 'by copying European works, the Mughal painter learnt to achieve spatial depth, realistic treatment of drapery and naturalistic facial expressions and gestures and sometimes a painterly modelling of the flesh'.[55]

Abu'l-Fadl, referring to the excellent technical and artistic quality of the works produced in Akbar's atelier, comparable to those of European art, commented: 'even inanimate objects look as if they had life'.[56] Increasingly stimulated by the realism expressed by Western paintings in the depiction of human beings and their emotions, Mughal artists 'strove to similarly observe human form and to achieve an unprecedented realism in its portrayal'.[57]

However, the emperor's pictorial tastes did not fit into the canons of Islamic art, as Islamic art prefers non-representational and stylized forms of expression to figurative and realistic ones. According to Islam, nature is a creation of God, but unlike Westerners who see in its beauty the presence of the divine spirit, Muslims see above all its transience. As a result, all phenomena are considered ephemeral, short-lived, and any attempt to reproduce them in images is useless. As a result, in Islamic painting, straightforward realism is completely rejected in favour of an iconoclastic tendency, giving rise to expressions characterized by abstract decorativism.[58] Moreover, the painter, especially the realist painter, would only assume, as we already know, a presumptuous attitude, due to his arrogant desire to compete with God's creative power.

Nevertheless, the Great Mughal, now increasingly determined to dismantle all such limiting beliefs, is reported to have said on one occasion:

> There are many that hate painting. But such men I dislike. It appears to me as if a painter had quite peculiar means of recognizing God; for a painter in sketching anything that has life, and in devising its limbs, one after the other, must come to feel that he cannot bestow individuality upon his work, and is thus forced to think of God, the giver of life, and will thus increase in knowledge.[59]

Akbar, therefore, could only agree with all the above arguments of the Jesuits in favour of a figurative art with a strict realist approach.[60] According to the art historian Bailey, 'Catholic art was perceived as universal because of its realism, and it was also seen as intensely spiritual. Unlike Islam, which had virtually no tradition of figurative devotional imagery and could not compete with Hindu iconography effectively. Catholic art possessed undeniable visual potency.'[61]

CHRISTIAN ART AT THE SERVICE OF THE SOVEREIGN'S LEGITIMIZATION

It would seem that the sovereign's interest was not only in Western painting styles and techniques. Many European travellers who visited his palaces were surprised by the number of rich and sumptuous frescoes and oil paintings depicting Christian subjects.[62]

According to some historians, the emperor's adoption of Christian figurative art was also part of the policy of legitimizing his power. In fact, the Mughals were a new dynasty and were well aware of their position as Muslim rulers of a conquered country, so as the Austrian scholar Ebba Koch states:

> they had to come to terms not only with their own Timurid–Islamic background but also with the strong and ancient culture of their Hindu

subjects. Furthermore, they had to establish their status as ruler vis-à-vis the Muslim dynasties, which ruled India before them and—of particular importance in our context—vis-à-vis the rulers of other countries.[63]

In a letter to King Philip II, Akbar argues for the existence of an affinity between all those who composed 'the exalted group of rulers who enjoy the noblest of distinction in consequence of a greater share of divine favour'.[64] According to the Great Mughal, the claims of such kinship were 'well-established among mighty potentates and acknowledged to be the chief conditions of amicable relations'.[65]

Ebba Koch further states that:

> This interest in European rulers included also an interest in their arts. The arts [...] were considered an important means of emphasizing the status of the ruler in the eyes of his subjects and of demonstrating superiority over other rulers. Not surprisingly, the Mughal emperors were keen to know how their European counterparts handled this issue.[66]

The Jesuits were particularly helpful in providing information to the Indian emperor on 'Christian principles', although their intent, at least initially, was his conversion to the Gospel.[67]

The first and foremost virtue that an Islamic ruler should possess, which somehow legitimizes him to rule, is justice. In Persian and Mughal panegyrics this virtue is indicated by a metaphor referring to the idea of the just ruler and the peaceful coexistence of domestic and wild animals under his rule.[68] The first gift offered by the Jesuits to the emperor, the Polyglot Bible of Antwerp, could not fail to amaze the court, as the image on the frontispiece is essentially a visual rendering of this metaphor.[69] In fact, it symbolically illustrates the peace between animals under the messianic ruler as announced by the prophet Isaiah (11: 6-9): two pairs of notoriously hostile animals (*a wolf and a lamb, a lion and an ox*) lie down and eat next to each other, consuming a herbivorous meal (pl. 3). In this particular context, the friendship between the animals indicates the *Pietatis Concordiæ*, the union of nations in the Christian faith (*unio christiana*) and the four languages in which the Old Testament appears in the Polyglot Bible.[70] This image inspired not only the depictions of Akbar's kingship (pl. 4), but also that of later emperors, notably Jahangir and Shah Jahan.

To complete the visual translation of the ideal sovereignty, the second frontispiece shows an image of *Pietas Regia* (pl. 5), represented here by a female figure wearing a laurel wreath supported by a putto, who hands her a palm. This allegory was intended to testify to the messianic role and

> the pietas of Philip II of Spain who presents himself as the guardian of the Catholic religion either with the sword (*aut gladio*) or with the word (*aut verbo*) while holding the polyglot Bible in his left hand and the heraldic insignia of Philip II in his right.[71]

Akbar, who was increasingly committed to the affirmation of his own person as a legitimate temporal (*'alam-i suri*) and spiritual (*'alam-i ma'nawi*) sovereign, certainly could not remain indifferent to this way of exalting the kingship of the Spanish sovereign, nor, according to the same Mughal sources, to the figure of the Pope, whom Bada'uni called *Mujtahid-i kamil*, i.e. the infallible authority in religious matters.[72] However, it was above all the emperor Jahangir who appreciated the symbolic potential of the representation of the Pietas Regia, and so, with a view to the visual legitimization of his power, imposed on his artists the use of this image as a model for the creation of some paintings, in which he himself appears at the centre instead of the female personification of royal virtue.[73]

Jesus and the Apostles

The *Pietas Regia* was certainly also the model for a Madonna and Child (pl. 6) by one of the most important Indian painters of the period, Basawan, who was of the Hindu faith but active in the ateliers of Akbar and Salim. He was impressed by the majesty of this Western woman, who echoed both a Hindu divinity and the mythical Mongol queen Alanqoa, considered the progenitor of the Mughals,[74] since, according to legend, she was impregnated by divine light, giving virgin birth to the patriarch of the Mongol royal line. The royal panegyrists and Abu'l-Fadl openly compared this queen to the Virgin Mary and Akbar's mother, who was called the *Maryam Makani* (Equal to Mary).[75] The figure of the Virgin Mary would thus embody a synthesis of Mongolian and Islamic culture and contribute to the process of legitimizing the power of the Mughals. The emperor and Prince Salim had ordered their artists to produce numerous paintings of Jesus and his mother. Mary is one of the most important characters in the Koran, in which she is the only woman mentioned by her own name, and the title of a Sūrah (the fourth) is dedicated to her.[76] By comparing his mother to the Virgin Mary, the Great Mughal was attempting to elevate his status to that of Christ.[77]

The Koran, no less, reserves a place of honour for Jesus: not only does it present him as a Muslim prophet, but it also gives him the title of Masih (Messiah), confirming, moreover, his chaste conception.[78] Jesus, in fact, was born miraculously at the behest of Allah, who created him in the womb of the Virgin Mary, as he had created Adam from a bit of earth.[79] The holy book, however, denies his death on the cross and the Resurrection, since he was not killed, but called by God to himself without facing the terrible trial of the Passion.

According to the great Andalusian mystic Ibn Arabi, Jesus deserves the title of *Khatam al-Awliya* (the Seal of Universal Holiness), as a perfect model of holy living[80] and as such is neither inferior nor superior to Muhammad, the *Khatam al-Anbiya* (the Seal of Prophecy).[81] Ibn Arabi's works inspired a form of devotion to the figure of the Koranic Jesus ('Isa ibn Maryam), practised by Emperor Akbar himself and many of his courtiers, especially his advisor Abu'l-Fadl.[82]

In Islamic literature, especially in Sufic literature, Jesus often appears as a strict ascetic, detached from the world, but surrounded by disciples (the Apostles) devoted to him. He represents the prototype of the spiritual guide, the perfect teacher (*shaikh al-kamil*), as well as being a model of goodness and meekness. In the Mughal palaces there were also numerous paintings of saints, especially the Apostles. The Apostles are respected by many Muslims for their dedication to Jesus and, according to an ancient Islamic tradition, converted to Islam retroactively. Sufis in particular honour the Apostles as models of their devotion to their teachers.[83]

As we know, Akbar, in order to strengthen the loyalty of courtiers and high officials towards him, had founded a sort of brotherhood, often called *Din-i-Ilahi* by historians, which was inspired by the master-disciple (*pir-murid*) relationship of the Sufism tradition.[84] As the French orientalist Louis Frédéric says, 'it is certain that Akbar wanted to create an elite who were devoted to him',[85] able to support him in his religious and social reforms.[86] The images of Jesus, the supreme *pir*, and the Apostles, his *murid*, depicted inside the palace, could be an effective symbol to arouse the devotion of the dignitaries towards the emperor.[87]

We can see how the figure of Jesus transcends the boundaries of Christianity: he is particularly loved by Muslims, but he can also be appreciated by Hindus. Hinduism often has a tendency to integrate traditions from other faiths. Frequently, foreign deities are incorporated into its pantheon, which is essentially complementary. It is not uncommon, especially today, to find Hindus worshipping images of Jesus Christ.[88] 'For them, Jesus is an *avatara*, someone who came down to earth, one of the many forms of manifestation of the supreme divinity.'[89] Akbar might have been aware of the potential of the Jesus figure as a meeting ground between Christians, Muslims and Hindus. Bailey observes: 'The Hindu context is especially important in a nation where Hindus formed the majority.'[90] The Canadian scholar also points out that certainly 'the Mughals chose Catholic imagery because Islam itself did not provide an iconographic tradition capable of combating the visually potent pantheon of Hindu deities'.[91]

We can conclude this topic with the words of art historian Ebba Koch:

> The Jesuit priests had taken along the pictures as a means to make the emperor perceive the realities of the Christian faith and the duties of the Christian ruler, to bring about eventually the Moghul's conversion to Christ—the great aim of the Mission. The Mughals accepted the means eagerly but used them as vehicles to represent the reality and the glory of their own dynasty and rule. The pictures, in the end, were used not *ad maiorem Dei gloriam*, but *ad maiorem Moguli gloriam*.[92]

A CHRISTIAN LITERATURE IN PERSIAN

As we may recall, it was previously argued that there were basically two main reasons why the emperor invited the Jesuits to his court: to collect a whole series of arguments against traditional Sunni hermeneutics and to have a valid aid for the activities of the *Maktab Khana*. It cannot be denied that Jerome Xavier proved to be able to respond positively to the Great Mughal's expectations, since his father, besides devoting himself to the translation of several biblical books and the composition of polemical writings of anti-Islamic content, was above all the author of a first Christian literature in the Persian language.

Looking at his oeuvre as a whole, it is possible to separate his works into several categories. A first group consists of treatises of a controversial nature, such as the *A'ina-yi haqq-numa* (The Mirror Showing the Truth) and its abridged and summarized version (*Muntakhab-i A'ina-yi haqq-numa*), which contain a systematic exposition as well as a comparison between Christian and Muslim doctrines.[93] Their aims are essentially apologetic, in that they seek to prove the superiority of the Christian religion.[94] In any case, these writings reflect the religious situation of the Mughal Empire and draw attention to the need for a thorough knowledge of Islam. They could also be understood as a sort of *vademecum* for the missionaries who went to the Mughal land.[95]

A second category includes some biographies: *Mir'at al-quds ya'ni dastan-i hazrat-i 'Isa* (The Mirror of Sanctity or the Life of the Lord Jesus), the *History of the Vicissitudes of the Apostles of the Lord Jesus and Commemoration of their Virtues*, the *Life of the Blessed Virgin* and the *Books of the Histories of some Saints*. These works form a single narrative and are based on texts taken from the Gospels and the Acts of the Apostles, but also on apocryphal and legendary sources. They have a popular character, which is why they proved to be useful in familiarizing the emperor and the court with the origin and history of Christianity and its protagonists.[96]

A third group concerns catechetical treatises, such as the *Bayan-i iman-i 'isawiyan* (Exposition of the Faith of Christians), a detailed commentary on the Creed, and a catechism written in Hindustani, while other works present non-essentially religious themes, such as the *Ababu's-saltanat* (The Duties of Kingship), a handbook of the duties of monarchical government.[97]

A 'Life of Jesus' in Persian

The *Mir'at al-quds ya'ni dastan-i hazrat-i 'Isa*[98] begins with an episode probably taken from the *Acts of Mar Mari*,[99] in which it is told that Abgar V, king of Edessa, when he was struck down by a very serious illness, sent his court painter to Jesus to paint him from life. Failing to do so, the distraught artist begged Christ to imprint his image on a piece of cloth. This miraculous portrait naturally led to the king's immediate recovery.[100] In highlighting this story, Xavier undoubtedly wanted to emphasize the importance of image worship in Christian life. Obviously, Abgar was also a clear reference to Akbar himself, since he too was a ruler who had sent embassies and artists in search of Catholic devotional images.[101]

The manuscript was richly decorated with miniatures by the artists of the imperial atelier, whose scenes in some cases seem to be inspired by the theatrical performances organized by the missionaries rather than by scriptural passages. In several illustrations one can recognize the Jesuits (pls. 1 and 2), who sometimes impersonated Jesus and other evangelical characters on stage.[102] Sometimes the Mughal artists, some of whom were also Hindus, adapted the Gospel scenes according to local stylistic forms. For example, according to the scholar Waraich, the image of

> *Jesus Asleep During a Storm at Sea* (pl. 9) resonates with numerous sculptural relief panels and paintings of the Hindu deity Vishnu sleeping on the cosmic water within cycles of time (pl. 10). Jesus is shown in a similar position as that of Vishnu, resulting in an unusually languorous pose, and both are surrounded by figures who attend to them, each with an attendant hovering above and another massaging their legs. Also striking that the sail of the boat where Jesus sleeps takes a form similar to the multi-headed cobra that provides shelter for Vishnu (pl. 11), a common form of representation across northern India.[103]

As for the text of the manuscript, according to Bailey it reflects a typically Jesuit way of representing biblical places and characters in a realistic way, a characteristic that can be traced back to the *compositio loci* (visual composition of place) of the 'Spiritual Exercises', a contemplative technique that makes use of the visual and imaginative element. Indeed, the book describes the facial characteristics of its main characters in great detail, as, for example, in the presentation of the Virgin Mary, which reads like a set of instructions for a portrait painter:[104]

> Mary was a girl of middling height and olive complexion, with a long face. Her eyes were large and tending to blue. Her hair was of a golden color. Her hands and fingers were long and well formed. In every feature she was well-proportioned. Her speech was extremely soft.[105]

The book offers similar descriptions of other characters, such as Jesus and John the Baptist. These reconstructions of sacred faces conceal a strategy of acculturation, as they echo the Islamic *hilya* tradition, i.e. the verbal descriptions of the face of the Prophet Muhammad, and the *shilpashastras*, which are texts describing the manual arts and the norms of Hindu religious iconography.[106]

XAVIER'S ANTI-ISLAMIC APOLOGETICS

Xavier's most important work is undoubtedly *A'ina-yi haqq-numa*, but it is a translation of an earlier treatise by the same author, entitled *Fuente de Vida*, written in Castilian, albeit with many lusisms.[107] The Roman Archive of the Society of Jesus preserves the only manuscript copy currently known, which was published in 2007 by the Instituto Ignacio de Loyola of the University of Deusto in a volume edited by Hugues Didier.

Following in the footsteps of the *Book of the Gentile and the Three Wise Men* by Ramon Llull (1233-1316), the work takes the form of a fictitious dialogue between a father, a *mullah* and a philosopher. The father is a Portuguese Jesuit, who would represent Xavier himself, although he was a Navarrese, or the Jesuits who resided at the court. The *mullah* is a Sunni theologian, not at all haughty and quite courteous. He reacts with surprising restraint to his father's attacks on Islamic dogma and Muhammad. His lack of aggression may reflect the vulnerable and minority position held by those still committed to the defence of Sunni orthodoxy in Akbar's court in the last period of his reign. The most interesting figure is that of the philosopher, culturally Muslim, but not a follower of Islam,[108] as he himself declares: 'I follow no prophet and am not bound by any Law. But I live according to what I understand in the philosophical teachings.'[109] This is probably a synthetic figure combining the traits of Akbar, Abu'l-Fadl and his brother, the poet Faydi, and Sufi free-thinkers or exponents of *Din-i-Ilahi*.[110]

Xavier's treatise was inspired by Ramon Llull's *Book of the Gentile and the Three Wise Men*, not only in its dialogue-like structure, but also in its recourse to the *rationes necessariae* to convince of the truth of Christianity.[111] Like Llull, the Jesuit is well aware of the fact that the Muslims deny the authority of Holy Scripture, which they consider to be falsified, and so he does not appeal to its authority, but resorts to the arguments of reason.[112]

In the first part of the *Fuente de Vida*, the main objective of the Christian interlocutor is to persuade the philosopher of the need for a religion revealed by God. A necessity that would be justified by a twofold observation: the inability of human intelligence to reach the Truth on its own and the inconceivable coexistence of a plurality of religions that claim to be equally true.[113] The religion that teaches us to know God, to love, adore and serve him is recognized as true. The Jesuit is now ready to demonstrate how the Christian faith is capable of meeting this criterion.

The following are the topics that most frequently recurred in the disputes between Christians and Muslims, such as the doctrines of the Trinity and the divinity of Christ, the Islamic dogma of the *tahrif* and the comparison between the law of Jesus and that of Muhammad.

The Holy Trinity and the Divinity of Christ

In *Fuente de Vida*, the divine oneness and trinity are defended against the accusation of tritheism, typical of Muslim religious controversy. In fact, the Koran conceives the trinitarian doctrine of Christians as a form of polytheism and accuses them of considering God, Jesus and Mary as three divinities, a concept blamed by the Koranic Jesus himself (Sūrah 5, 116). Fakhr al-din Razi (1149-1209), one of the foremost scholars of the Koran of the classical period, quietly states that he has never known any Christian to claim that Mary was part of the Trinity, so this misleading conception could refer to an extinct Christian sect.[114] According to the scholar W. Montgomery Watt: 'The idea that Mary was one of the Trinity may have come from an obscure set of Collyridians, heard of in Arabia more than two centuries before Muhammad. It is also possible that there was confusion due to the fact that in some Semitic languages the word for Spirit is feminine.'[115]

In the Koran, the Holy Spirit never appears in the Christian trinitarian triad. The Jesuit, however, illustrates the divine processions in a scholastic exposition, but in the explanation of the generation of the Son from the Father he feels compelled to resort initially to the expression 'Word of God'—also Koranic—because he is aware that the Muslims understand 'Son of God' in a carnal sense. Consequently, he insists on the spiritual meaning of the name and expounds the procession of the Second Person through the analogy with the human soul, recalling the Augustinian-Thomistic conception.[116]

The Jesuit also states that Muhammad himself, by attributing to Christ the titles of 'Spirit of God' and 'Word of God', without knowing it or wanting it, would have confessed his divine filiation.[117] According to the experts, however, the personal character of the Word is not evident in the Koran; on the contrary, according to the precise observation of the scholar Maria Gallo, already quoted above:

> Jesus is the Word and Spirit of God only because his birth from a virgin mother is the fruit of the creative 'Word of God' as is the life received by the first man Adam as a result of that word and that vital breath of which the first two chapters of Genesis speak.[118]

Similarly, the exegete Joachim Gnilka states that the passages of the Koran in which Jesus is attributed the title of 'Word of God' 'have nothing in common with the New Testament Christology of the Logos, according to which Christ is the eternally pre-existent Logos of God (Jn 1:1), but rather emphasize the creative power of God'.[119]

The accusation of tahrif

As we can remember Jews and Christians are blamed by Muslims for falsifying their scriptures. The Torah, the Psalter and the Gospel originally had a message that corresponded to that contained in the Koran. Therefore, everything in the Bible that does not coincide with the holy book of Islam is considered altered. The father of the Fuente de Vida wonders on what valid basis this accusation is made. Are the Muslims able to provide proof of the alleged forgery? Are they in possession of the unaltered biblical text? And why have they never shown it? To say that it has been lost seems simplistic to say the least.[120] According to the Jesuit, behind the accusation of *tahrif*, there is an attempt to hide an obvious reality: the actual dependence of the Koran on Jewish and Christian materials and traditions. In this way, the accusation of scriptural alteration,[121] which was deliberately formulated to discredit Jews and Christians, is unexpectedly overturned towards Muslims. Xavier confirms the hypothesis of the existence of a 'proto-Koran',[122] with profoundly Christian content: 'Those who succeeded your prophet have changed many things, contradicting the true Koran.'[123] Is this alteration the result of deliberate omissions or distracting errors by later copyists?[124] Didier writes that for Xavier: 'the original redaction core of the holy book of Islam is a Christian text, but under the influence of various necessities, especially political, this originally good and just text has been transformed or more precisely perverted'.[125]

An indication of the corruption of the original message would be, for example, the presence in the Koran of a more permissive morality, as far as hedonism is concerned, which would benefit men but be to the detriment of women.[126]

Xavier was not the only one who understood Islam as a deviation from the Christian religious tradition. Many scholars and erudites of the present and the past have raised such a possibility. Akbar himself was aware of a tradition about a mysterious Christian who allegedly helped the Prophet to compose the Koran.[127] As many will know, there are numerous points of connection between the Koran and the Bible. Indeed, it is possible that Muhammad had contacts with some Jewish, Judeo-Christian and Gnostic communities in the Near East, but also with Nestorians and Monophysites who had settled in Arabia following the condemnation of their heresies by the Councils of Ephesus (431) and Chalcedon (451). The biblical echoes present in the Koran would therefore depend rather on frequenting these groups than on direct access to Holy Scripture. Recently, a Lebanese researcher, Joseph Azzi, supported the thesis that an Ebionite priest was Muhammad's spiritual master,[128] while Joachim Gnilka even claims that Islam was formed within a Judeo-Christian community.[129] The French scholar Alfred-Louis de Prémare, on the other hand, grants Syriac Christianity an essential role in the genesis of the Koran.[130]

It is, however, difficult to discern which of these monotheistic religious traditions had the greatest influence on Muhammad's spiritual formation. In any case, it is probable that, faced with the profound divergences between the monotheistic currents, he became convinced of the existence of an original faith to which all these versions would refer or from which they would derive; a faith that would now appear unrecognizable due to the continuous alterations it had undergone. In essence, Muhammad's aim was to re-establish the hanif, the 'pure religion', the 'uncontaminated monotheistic cult as practised by Abraham.'[131]

'Islamic superiority'?

Muslims consider Muhammad as the 'seal of prophecy' affixed to the ultimate Revelation. Hence the previous monotheistic religions are destined to give way before the last and most perfect religion of God for all mankind. In practice, Islam would constitute the overcoming, indeed the abrogation of Christianity and Judaism. According to Xavier, it is not difficult to dismantle this claim to superiority: a simple comparison between the lives and teachings of Jesus and Muhammad and the religious systems derived from them allows one to recognize the absolute pre-eminence of Christianity.

The Jesuit of *Fuente de Vida*, in his enumeration and explanation of the ten biblical commandments, intends to highlight their superiority over the precepts contained in the Koran and the *Hadith*, which

Muhammad, in order to attract converts to his religion, wanted to be more permissive and less demanding. In particular, Islam is lenient towards those behaviours that are directly opposed to a virtuous life, such as the practice of concealing the faith in dangerous circumstances, violence and revenge against enemies and infidels and the lack of control over sexual impulses or passions.[132]

A strong powerful judgement is expressed against the principle of *taqiyya* or *kitman* (dissimulation), recognized and permitted by Koranic law, which 'authorises the believer, whose life is threatened, to dissimulate his religious affiliation or pretend to embrace another one',[133] with the promise to subsequently do *tawba*, that is, penance.[134] In *Fuente de Vida*, the father reminds the *mullah* of his fundamental moral obligation to bear witness to what he judges to be the truth.[135]

> Professing one's religion is necessary [...]. [Christ] commands us to profess that he is our leader and guide and that we profess his religion, should we give our lives for this [...]. [On the contrary] in your Koran, your Prophet tells you that when you find yourself in a difficult situation, you say: 'For you is your religion, and for me is my religion' [Sūrah 109: 6]. Does this seem to you a good profession of faith? But it is to show that for you there may be another good religion, beyond the one you have.[136]

According to the Jesuit, Islam combines violence and the concealment of truth: 'Your religion says to you, as far as professing it is concerned: kill. Ours says to us, as far as professing it is concerned, die. Yours says to you, when you cannot kill or punish: hide and speak so as to please men.'[137]

As we can understand, there is a profound difference between Christian and Muslim doctrine, as the former exhorts us not only to bear witness to our faith, even where it may cost us our lives, but also to be magnanimous and forgiving towards our enemies. Islam spread through Muhammad's and his successors' bloody policy of territorial expansion and the associated forced conversions of subjugated populations. Christianity, on the other hand, thanks the example and sacrifice of its preachers. In Islam, the faithful are incited to violence and hatred towards those who do not adhere to their religion, adopting measures of clemency only towards those who convert or pay tribute.[138] Jesus' teaching is in agreement with reason and divine law because it is inflexibly opposed to the violent methods used in conversion, in which, instead, freedom should play a decisive role.[139]

In the Koran and the *Hadith* there are also numerous phrases that clearly incite to revenge and therefore

> under the pretext of religion, he gives you licence to do whatever harm you can do to those you consider enemies [...]. Your Prophet [...] commands you to punish those who offend, that you should tear out their eyes for an eye and a tooth for a tooth, provided that you do not exaggerate [Sūrah 5: 45].[140]

Consequently, since Muslim law encourages warfare and revenge, it seems rather reminiscent of

> a regulation for soldiers, who like to take revenge, rather than for men who have to suppress their appetites in order not to deviate from the measure dictated by reason. And it was useless for your Prophet to teach such a doctrine, for nature itself teaches vengeance, without the need for masters or prophets.[141]

According to Xavier, Islam essentially represents a regression from Christianity, and this can be seen especially in the private sexual and emotional sphere. Long before the advent of Christ, the practice of polygamy by the Patriarchs was due to a special dispensation from God, perhaps permitted as a means of multiplying the chosen people, while the libel of repudiation was granted by Moses to the Jews because of the hardness of their hearts (Mt 19: 8). Jesus then, appealing to the original will of God, re-established monogamous and indissoluble marriage, emphasizing the equal rights of man and woman. In this respect, it is evident that Islam has brought about a backward step by granting the head of the family four legitimate wives and an indeterminate number of slave concubines.[142]

Polygamy leads to a flagrant disparity that escapes the dignity and rights of women: 'it seems that it is an immense inequality that your Law establishes between man and woman. Indeed, it grants the man so many licences to live according to his own pleasure and it shakes so many hands with the woman.'[143]

In this respect, it is already possible to see 'the perfection of the Gospel in relation to the religion [...] of Muslims, and how unreasonable it is to say that the Law of Mohammed and his Koran abrogates the Gospel'.[144]

Muhammad: 'Seal of Prophecy'?

The Jesuit of *Fuente de Vida* states that if Muhammad claims the status of 'seal of prophecy' for himself, he must have surpassed Jesus in holiness of life, miracles and influence. In the Koran, Christ is always spoken of with great reverence: a man full of holiness and without sin, referred to as the 'spirit of God', as he was conceived like Adam by the spirit and power of God. He was the son of Mary, the most virtuous of all women, and became one of the greatest prophets, performing extraordinary miracles during his mission.[145] Many events in the life of Jesus were predicted by the prophets of the Old Testament, while regarding Muhammad there is no prediction to be found in the Holy Scriptures.[146]

Christ was born of the Blessed Virgin without human intervention but by the power of God and descended from Abraham on the line of Isaac, the son of Sarah, the patriarch's wife. Muhammad's father and mother, on the other hand, were his parents in the common sense of the term and, although included in an Abrahamic genealogy, were descended from Ishmael, the outcast son born of Abraham's carnal union with the slave Hagar, who, after his removal, disappears in the biblical account as if he had never been there.[147] The Revelation of Jesus constitutes the direct continuation and fulfilment of the Old Testament Revelation; Muhammad feels invested with continuity with the Jewish-Christian tradition, a continuity which, however, does not exist.

The father then compares the conduct of the two prophets, especially with regard to the sexual sphere. Jesus chose a life of perfect chastity, while Muhammad seems to have shown a certain sexual incontinence. So he allowed himself a dispensation from the already particularly permissive precepts, going so far as to have thirteen or fifteen wives and seventeen concubines or slaves. Not content with this, he claimed other privileges such as the following: a husband had to repudiate his wife if she wanted to be united with the prophet. In this way, Muhammad could also legitimize his marriage to Zainab, wife of his adopted son Zaid. The Jesuit wonders at this point whether it is possible to believe that these privileges were granted by God. The *mullah* tries to defend his prophet by again using the argument of the polygamy of the patriarchs. According to the father, special circumstances permitted such an exception, but these did not exist for long when Christ came into the world and restored monogamy. Polygamy was allowed only to a limited extent for the multiplication of offspring, when the chosen people constituted a tiny minority compared to pagan civilizations. Muhammad, on the other hand, had only had two sons by all his wives who died in their infancy. The *mullah* still tries to defend Muhammad by stating that the last of the prophets should have no successors, as Muslim sages teach. This intervention only confirms the accusation made by his father: Muhammad was only influenced by passion.[148]

The *mullah* then appeals to the numerous miracles, which according to tradition were performed by Muhammad. The father intervenes, denying their authenticity and stating that the Koran itself does not attribute any to the prophet. He also points out that they are pseudo-miracles, unrealistic and not true at all, such as when a tree split in two to let Muhammad pass, reuniting immediately afterwards, or ridiculous and even immoral such as his superhuman sexual performances. By contrast, the miracles of Jesus recounted in the Gospels, some of which are confirmed in the Koran, appear sober, not sensationalist.[149] 'Jesus does not perform miracles to show off his prodigious energies or to satisfy the morbidity of the curious or to win the sympathy of powerful.'[150]

The *mullah* states, however, that the real miracle of Islam would be the Koran itself, in its inimitability and insuperability: an irrefutable proof of its divine origin.[151] In addition to its content, its religious message, the Koranic miracle would consist in its literary beauty, since no human being would be able to compose something similar.[152] According to Xavier, the excellence of a book depends on an orderly arrangement of topics, dealt with logically, with high content and with extreme coherence of thought. The holy book of Islam, however, does not seem to meet any of these requirements.[153]

Finally, the Jesuit also points out that the warlike attitude of the prophet of Islam and his hatred of his enemies are in open contrast to the meekness that Jesus showed throughout his public life, especially during the moments of his passion. But it is above all another substantial difference that deserves to be underlined: in the Koran itself it is claimed that Muhammad is dead and that, on the contrary, Jesus is still alive.[154]

The long confrontation between Muhammad and Jesus seems to have brought out sufficient synergistic elements to undermine the figure of the founder of Islam. Akbar, as we know, on the basis of political motivations, but also induced by personal convictions matured over time, aimed at adapting the Muslim religion to Indo-Iranian culture, through a process of de-absolutization and relativization of dogmas. The Fuente de Vida with its arguments could certainly represent a decisive contribution to the questioning of the superiority status of Sunni Islam and the image of Muhammad as the restorer of God's primitive revelation. Having demonstrated the superiority of Christ over Muhammad, the latter could no longer be presented as the definitive prophet. In this way, Akbar would have had the opportunity to claim the exercise of a prophetic role and of a religious legislator, which would also have allowed him to no longer be subject to the Koranic Law and to escape forever the control of the *ulama*.[155]

The emperor had inaugurated at the court a Sufic-inspired form of devotion to Jesus, the prototype of universal holiness. In a way, the Fuente de Vida only confirmed Christ to the sovereign as the one and only true model of kingship, an operation carried out in parallel, as we know, by the painters of the imperial studio. Jesus is honoured by Muslims as a great prophet, but he can also be welcomed by Hindus as a spiritual master or even as an *avatar* of a deity. This is because he is a universal figure, potentially representing for all men, regardless of their adherence to the faith, one of the highest peaks of human nature. So Akbar could not have chosen a different emblem to represent his sovereignty.

NOTES

1. K. Lè Thành, *Islam*, p. 127.
2. E. Fasana, 'Introduzione', p. 11.
3. O. Saaidia, 'L'évangélisation des musulmans, mission impossible?', J. Pirotte (ed.), *Résistances à l'évangélisation. Interprétations historiques et enjeux théologiques* (Paris: Karthala, 2004), pp. 257, 263-4.
4. H. Didier, 'Ormuz', p. 165.
5. *Hadith* attributed to Muhammad, quoted in S.A. Rahman, *Punishment of Apostasy in Islam* (Selangor: The Other Press Sdn Bhd), pp. 58-9.
6. O. Saaidia, 'L'évangélisation des musulmans', pp. 258, 263.
7. Ibid.
8. Ibid., p. 265.
9. P. Branca, *Pagine di letteratura araba* (Milan: EDUCatt, 2009), p. 35.
10. C. Saccone, *I percorsi dell'Islam. Dall'esilio di Ismaele alla rivolta dei nostri giorni* (Padua: Messaggero, 2003), p. 279.
11. O. Saadia, 'L'évangélisation des musulmans', p. 265.
12. *Hadith* attributed to Muhammad, quoted in I.R. Al-Faruqi, *Islam and Other Faiths* (Leicester: Islamic Foundation 1998), p. 237.
13. O. Saadia, 'L'évangélisation des musulmans', p. 265.
14. E. Fasana, 'Introduzione', p. 11.
15. O. Saadia, 'L'évangélisation des musulmans', pp. 267-8.
16. S. Waraich, 'Competing and Complementary Visions of the Court of the Great Mogor', in D. Leibsohn and J. Favrot Peterson (eds), *Seeing Across Cultures in the Early Modern World* (Farnham: Ashgate, 2012), p. 79.
17. As the Italian scholar Emanuele Colombo says, Alessandro Valignano (1539-1606), Visitor General of the East India missions, 'realised the need to identify men capable of withstanding enormous physical exertion, with the cultural background necessary to live in contact with advanced civilisations' and 'willing to learn the complex languages of the East in a reasonable time' (E. Colombo, *Convertire i musulmani. L'esperienza di un gesuita spagnolo del Seicento* [Turin: Bruno Mondadori, 2007], p. 4).
18. A. Camps, *Jerome Xavier*, pp. 184-5; and M. Debergh, 'Premiers jalons de l'évangélisation de l'Inde, du Japon et de la Chine', in J.M. Mayeur, C. Pietri, A. Vauchez and M. Venard (eds), *Histoire du Christianisme*, vol. VIII, *Le temps des confessions (1530-1620)* (Paris: Desclée, 1992), pp. 803-4.

19. G.A. Bailey, 'The Truth-Showing Mirror: Jesuit Catechism and the Arts in Mughal India', in J.W. O'Malley, G.A. Bailey, S.J. Harris and T.F. Kennedy (eds), *The Jesuits: Cultures, Sciences, and the Arts, 1540-1773* (Toronto: University of Toronto Press, 1999), p. 391.
20. Y. Moubarak, *Recherches sur la pensée chrétienne et l'Islam dans les temps modernes et à l'époque contemporaine* (Beirut: Université libanaise, 1977), pp. 224-5.
21. G.A. Bailey, 'The Truth-Showing Mirror', p. 391.
22. G. Amaladass and G. Lowner, *Christian Themes in Indian Art: From the Mogul Times till Today* (New Delhi: Manohar, 2012), pp. 74, 79, 85.
23. G.A. Bailey, 'The Truth-Showing Mirror', p. 392.
24. Ibid.
25. Jesuit *accommodation* is a subject that has provoked and still provokes debate among scholars. This is not the place to examine the different positions. For the moment, we can at least present the essence of this missionary method in the words of historian Paola Vismara:

    The Jesuits distinguished themselves by the novelty of their method, called 'accommodation' or 'adaptation'. In fact, they proposed to insert themselves within the local cultures, taking on those characteristics that were not considered incompatible with the essence of the Christian message: this message had to be translated within the cultural, philosophical and religious categories typical of the local tradition (P. Vismara, 'Il cattolicesimo dalla "riforma cattolica" all'assolutismo', in G. Filoramo and D. Menozzi [eds], *Storia del cristianesimo,* III. *L'età moderna* [Bari: Laterza, 1997], p. 191).

    The following volumes can be consulted for an initial in-depth study of the subject: E. Colombo, 'Gesuitomania. Studi recenti sulle missioni gesuitiche (1540-1773)', in M. Catto, G. Mongini and S. Mostaccio (eds), *Evangelizzazione e Globalizzazione. Le missioni gesuitiche nell'età moderna tra storia e storiografia* (Rome: Società Editrice Dante Alighieri, 2010), pp. 49-52; and B. Majorana, 'Tra carità e cultura. Formazione e prassi missionaria nella Compagnia di Gesù', in P. Broggio, F. Cantù, P.A. Fabre and A. Romano (eds), *I gesuiti ai tempi di Claudio Acquaviva*, pp. 226-31.
26. Y. Moubarak, *Recherches*, p. 223.
27. D. Cocozza, *Cristo: Un profeta tra Bibbia e Corano* (Rome: Editoria scientifica, 2008), p. 7; P. Marzolo, 'Saggio sui segni', in *Annali delle Università toscane* (Pisa: Tipografia Editrice Cav. F. Mariotti, 1867),

p. 91; and M. Rizzi, *Le prime traduzioni del Corano in Italia* (Turin: L'Harmattan Italia, 2007), p. 28.
28. A. Camps, *Jerome Xavier*, pp. 185-8; and Y. Moubarak, *Recherches*, p. 223.
29. H. Didier, *Famómes d'Islam et de Chine*, p. 246.
30. A letter from Jerome Xavier to Claudio Acquaviva, Lahore, 20 August 1595, quoted in J. Wicki (ed.), *Documenta Indica*, vol. XVII, p. 70.
31. A letter from Manoel Pinheiro to João Alvarez, Lahore, 3 September 1595, quoted in G. Peruschi, *Informatione*, p. 57.
32. P.M. Carvalho, '"Rarities from Goa" at the Courts of Humayun, Akbar and Jahangir (1530-1627)', in J. Flores and N. Vassallo e Silva (eds), *Goa and the Great Mughal*, pp. 103-6.
33. S. Stronge, 'Il Libro di Akbar', p. 25; and G. Amaladass and G. Lowner, *Christian Themes in Indian Art*, p. 44.
34. J. Britschgi, 'Alcuni aspetti della pittura', p. 67.
35. H. Didier, 'Le role de l'iconographie dans les missions jésuites (Inde du nord et Tibet, XVIe-XVIIe siècles)', in J. Pirotte, C. Sappia and O. Servais (eds), *Images et diffusion du christianisme: Expressions graphiques en contexte missionnaire XVIe-XXe siècles* (Lyon: Karthala, 2012), p. 45.
36. R. Oliveira Lopes, *Arte e Alteridade. Confluencias da Arte Cristà na India, na China e no Japào, séc. XVI a XVIII*, Ph.D. thesis in Fine Arts (Lisbon: University of Lisbon, 2011), p. 229.
37. Cardinal Gabriele Paleotti (1522-1597), for example, in his *Discorso intorno alle imagini sacre e profane*, states that often, in books, it happens that what is learned with great difficulty is easily forgotten; where images engrave what they teach so solidly in the tables of memory that it remains printed there for many years. And furthermore, images in a small space, without turning volumes or sheets, contain very broad and very deep concepts (quoted in P. Barocchi, *Trattati d'arte del Cinquecento*, vol. II [Bari: G. Laterza, 1961], p. 222).
From a pedagogical and catechetical point of view, the usefulness of images for the education of people in the Christian faith could be recognized because of their particularity of being a book open to everyone's abilities, composed of a language common to all kinds of people: men, women, children, adults, scholars, ignorant people; and yet they are understood [...] by all nations, and by all minds, without recourse to pedagogues or interpreters (ibid., p. 223).
38. J. Xavier, *Fuente de Vida. Tratado Apologético dirigido al Rey Mogol de la India en 1600* (San Sebastian: Universidad de Duesto, 2007), p. 329.
39. E. Devapriam, 'Repercussions of the Counter: Reformation on the

Works of the Mughal and the Florentine Painters Realism in the late Sixteenth and early Seventeenth Centuries', in D. Jones (ed.), *A Mirror of Princes: The Mughals and the Medici* (Mumbai: Marg Publications, 1987), p. 154. 'The *Spiritual Exercises* [o]f Ignatius Loyola [...] encourages the worshipper in prayer to use his five senses to vividly "realize" and "represent" the subject on which his spirit is focusing' (ibid.). In the two Prefaces to the *Adnotationes et Meditationes in Evangelia* by Jerónimo Nadal (1507-80), a work that was also presented to the Mughal court, it is stated that:

> the illustrations were to be used as an aid to meditation. Thus the 'art preceded the calling up of mental images'. This Jesuit notion of 'realistic awareness of the subjects' in meditation surely would have affected the artistic taste of the period (ibid.).

40. E. Koch, 'The Influence of the Jesuit Mission', p. 22.
41. Except with regard to the representation of idols.
42. F. Boespflug, *Dieu et ses images. Une histoire de l'éternel dans l'art* (Paris: Bayard, 2008), p. 45.
43. R. Ettinghausen, *La peinture arabe* (Geneva: Skira, 1962), p. 12.
44. Ibid., pp. 12-13.
45. A. Besançon, *L'image interdite. Une histoire intellectuelle de l'iconoclasme* (Paris: Fayard, 1994), p. 115.
46. S. Hoyland and S.N. Banerjee (eds), *The Commentary of Father Monserrate*, p. 138.
47. F. Guerreiro, *Relagam annual das Cousas que fizeram os padres da Companhia de Iesus na India, & Iapão nos annos de 600. & 601. & do processo de conversão, & Christandade daquellas partes,* quoted in G.A. Bailey, 'The Indian Conquest of Catholic Art: The Mughals, the Jesuits, and Imperial Mural Painting', *Art Journal*, vol. 57, no. 1 (1998), p. 30. As in the thirty-fifth session of the Council of Trent (1563), the use of images had been clearly defined and sanctioned 'because the honour which is shown them is referred to the prototypes which those images represent' (Council of Trent, Decree *on the Invocation, Veneration, and Relics of Saints, and n Sacred Images*).
48. G.A. Bailey, 'The Truth-Showing Mirror', p. 388.
49. S. Waraich, 'Competing and Complementary Visions', p. 86.
50. Ibid., p. 77.
51. Abu'l-Fadl, *Ain-i-Akbari*, vol. I (Calcutta: G.M. Rouse, 1873), p. 107.
52. E. Wellez, *Akbar's Religious Thought Reflected in Mogul Painting* (London: George Allen and Unwin Ltd, 1952), pp. 1, 29.

53. E. Devapriam, 'Repercussions of the Counter-Reformation', p. 156.
54. J. Britschgi, 'Alcuni aspetti della pittura', p. 67.
55. E. Devapriam, 'Repercussions of the Counter-Reformation', p. 156.
56. Abu'l-Fadl, *Ain-i-Akbari*, quoted in ibid.
57. Ibid.
58. S.A. Surme, *Kurdistan. Storia, economia e risorse, società e tradizioni, arte e cultura, religione* (Bologna: Pendragon, 1998), p. 66.
59. Abu'l-Fadl, *Ain-i-Akbari*, quoted in M. Malik, *History of India* (New Delhi: New Saraswati House, 2016), p. 226.
60. E. Koch, 'Pietre Dure and other Artistic Contacts between the Court of the Mughals and that of the Medici', in D. Jones (ed.), *A Mirror of Princes*, p. 30.
61. G.A. Bailey, *The Jesuits and the Grand Mogul: Renaissance Art at the Imperial Court of India, 1580-1630* (Washington: Smithsonian Institution, 1998), p. 38.
62. Id., 'The Indian Conquest of Catholic Art', p. 24.
63. E. Koch, 'Pietre Dure', p. 30.
64. A letter from Akbar to King Philip II of 1582, quoted in ibid.
65. Ibid.
66. Ibid.
67. Ibid.
68. Ibid., p. 52. For example, the Persian panegyrist Muhammad Khwandamir (1475-1534), who also worked at the Mughal court, wrote of Emperor Humayun:

    Under the protection and shelter of his justice deer sleep carelessly in the lap of panthers, and fish fearlessly take rest near crocodiles; pigeons become friends of falcons and sparrows chirp fearlessly in front of eagles. Under his just administration deer in the forest go abreast with the male lion; the waterfowl tells its secrets to the hawk; the pigeon relates its story to the falcon (Muhammad Khwandamir, *Qanun-i Humayuni*, quoted in E. Koch, 'The Influence of the Jesuit Mission', p. 18.)

69. E. Koch, 'Pietre Dure', p. 52.
70. Id., 'The Influence of the Jesuit Mission', pp. 16-17.
71. V. Fortunati Pietrantonio, *La Pittura in Emilia e in Romagna*, I. *Il Cinquecento: un'avventura artistica tra natura e idea* (Bologna: Nuova Alfa, 1994), p. 116.
72. E. Koch, 'The Influence of the Jesuit Mission', p. 28.
73. Ibid., pp. 19-20.
74. P. Madhok, 'Christian–Islamic Relations in the Court Art of Mughal

Indian', *The International Journal of the Arts in Society*, vol. 4 (2010), p. 6.

75. Ibid., p. 12; and G.A. Bailey, *Art on the Jesuit Missions in Asia and Latin America, 1542-1773* (Toronto: University of Toronto Press, 1999), p. 138.
76. Ibid.
77. P. Madhok, 'Christian–Islamic Relations', p. 12.
78. Ibid., pp. 12-13; and G.A. Bailey, *Art on the Jesuit Missions*, p. 137.
79. J.M. Abd el-Jalil, *Testimone del Corano e del Vangelo* (Milan: Jaca Book, 2006), p. 130.
80. In Sufism, holiness means divine closeness, divine friendship, or mystical union with God.
81. F. Skali, *Gesù nella tradizione sufi* (Milan: Paoline, 2007), p. 45; and C. Saccone, *I percorsi dell'Islam*, p. 127.
82. H. Didier, 'Les jésuites auprès du Grand Mogol Akbar', p. 29; and id., 'Ormuz', p. 174.
83. G.A. Bailey, *Art on the Jesuit Missions*, pp. 137-9.
84. Ibid., pp. 139-40.
85. L. Frédéric, *Akbar le Grand Moghol*, p. 273.
86. Ibid.
87. G.A. Bailey, *Art on the Jesuit Missions*, p. 140.
88. H. Hanggi, 'Come gli Indù vedono Gesù Cristo', *Communio: Rivista internazionale di Teologia e Cultura*, vol. 213 (2007), p. 29.
89. Ibid.
90. G.A. Bailey, 'The Indian Conquest of Catholic Art', p. 29.
91. Ibid.
92. E. Koch, 'The Influence of the Jesuit Mission', p. 29.
93. A. Camps, *Jerome Xavier*, p. 192.
94. E. MacLagan, *The Jesuits and the Great Mogul*, pp. 206-7.
95. A. Camps, *Jerome Xavier*, p. 193.
96. Ibid., p. 194.
97. Ibid., p. 195.
98. This work by Xavier on the life of Christ is quoted in *Von Reimarus zu Wrede: Eine Geschichte der Leben-Jesu-Forschung* by the well-known and multifaceted scholar Albert Schweitzer (1875-1965), who writes:

    The only interesting Life of Jesus written before Reimarus, was composed by a Jesuit in Persian. The author was the Indian missionary Hieronymus Xavier, nephew of Francis Xavier, and it was designed for the use of Akbar, the Moghul Emperor, who, in the latter part of the sixteenth century, had become the most powerful potentate in Hindustan. (A. Schweitzer, *The Quest of the Historical Jesus* [North Chelmsford: Courier Corporation, 2012], pp. 13-14.)

99. It is an account narrating the story of Apostle Mari, who was initially a disciple of Addai in Edessa and was then sent by him to preach in Persia (M. Casadei, 'La Siria, terra di missione nella Didascalia di Addai. Il viaggio e l'apostolo', in *Quaderni di storia religiosa*, vol. 13 [2006], p. 95).
100. J. Xavier, *Mir'at al-quds (Mirror of Holiness): A Life of Christ for Emperor Akbar* (Leiden: Brill, 2012), p. 139.
101. G.A. Bailey, 'The Truth-Showing Mirror', p. 395. 'Akbar' and 'Abgar' in Persian have the same four letters (ibid.). In fact, as early as 1575 Akbar had sent an embassy to Goa led by Haji Habibullah. Among other objectives, it was also to acquire artistic and cultural goods of Catholic inspiration (S. Stronge, 'Il Libro di Akbar', pp. 23-4).
102. G.A. Bailey, 'The Truth-Showing Mirror', p. 391.
103. S. Waraich, 'Competing and Complementary Visions', pp. 84-5.
104. G.A. Bailey, *Art on the Jesuit Missions*, p. 129.
105. J. Xavier, *Mir'at al-quds*, p. 145.
106. G.A. Bailey, *Art on the Jesuit Missions*, pp. 129-30.
107. H. Didier, *Jerónimo Xavier*, p. 151.
108. Id., 'Muslim Heterodoxy', pp. 919-21.
109. J. Xavier, *Fuente de Vida*, p. 91.
110. H. Didier, 'Muslim Heterodoxy', pp. 920-1.
111. M. Debergh, 'Premiers Jalons', p. 806.
112. H. Didier, *Fantomes d'Islam et de Chine*, p. 243.
113. Y. Moubarac, *Recherches*, pp. 219-20; and H. Didier, *Fantomes d'Islam et de Chine*, p. 243.
114. C.W. Troll, *Domande islamiche. Risposte cristiane* (Brescia: Queriniana, 2010), pp. 62-3.
115. W.M. Watt, *Muslim–Christian Encounters: Perceptions and Misperceptions* (London: Routledge, 2013), p. 23.
116. A. Camps, *Jerome Xavier*, p. 108.

    Just as we, when we think, cause a concept, an idea, an image or a mental verb to proceed from us, so, on the basis of what Revelation says, we must say that God, in thinking Himself, causes a Word to proceed from Himself in everything identical with Himself. With the difference, however, with respect to us that in God the Word is substantial while in us it is accidental, so that in God the procession of the Word is also a generation, and the Second Person is not only Word, but also Son. (R. Goggi, 'Introduzione alla Questione 4', in San Tommaso d'Aquino, *Le questioni disputate*, vol. I [Bologne: Edizioni Studio Domenicano, 1992], p. 406.)

117. A. Camps, *Jerome* Xavier, p. 112.
118. M. Gallo, *Omelia arabo-cristiana dell'VIII secolo*, p. 61.
119. J. Gnilka, *Bibbia e Corano* (Milan: Àncora, 2006), p. 91.
120. A. Camps, *Jerome Xavier*, pp. 117-21.
121. H. Didier, *Fantòmes d'Islam et de Chine*, pp. 241-2.
122. Id., 'Muslim Heterodoxy', p. 903.
123. J. Xavier, *Fuente de Vida*, p. 344.
124. H. Didier, 'Muslim Heterodoxy', p. 903.
125. Id., 'Jérome Xavier, critique de l'éthique musulmane dans Fuente de Vida, au nom de la dignité de la femme', in M.T. Urvoy (ed.), *Christianisme et islam. Foi et Loi* (Versailles: Éditions de Paris, 2010), p. 73.
126. Ibid.
127. Id., *Fantòmes d'Islam et de Chine*, p. 241.
128. J. Azzi, *Le Prétre et le Prophéte. Aux sources du Coran* (Paris: M&L, 2004), pp. 100-9.
129. J. Gnilka, *Die Nazarener und der Koran. Eine Spurensuche* (Freiburg im Breisgau: Herder Verlag Gmbh, 2007).
130. A.L. de Prémare, *Les fondations de l'Islam. Entre écriture et histoire* (Paris: Seuil, 2002), pp. 242-77.
131. A.M. Di Noia, *Maometto* (Rome: Newton Compton, 2012), p. 32.
132. A. Camps, *Jerome Xavier*, p. 128.
133. S. Mervin, *L'Islam. Fondamenti e dottrine* (Milan: Pearson Italia, 2004), p. 76.
134. J. Xavier, *Fuente de Vida*, p. 376.
135. H. Didier, *Jérome Xavier*, p. 76.
136. J. Xavier, *Fuente de Vida*, pp. 374-5.
137. Ibid., p. 376.
138. Ibid., pp. 375-7.
139. A. Camps, *Jerome Xavier*, pp. 129-32.
140. J. Xavier, *Fuente de Vida*, p. 379.
141. Ibid., p. 384.
142. A. Camps, *Jerome Xavier*, pp. 129-32.
143. J. Xavier, *Fuente de Vida*, p. 395.
144. Ibid., p. 391.
145. A. Camps, *Jerome Xavier*, p. 139.
146. Ibid.

147. Ibid., p. 140.
148. Ibid., pp. 141-5.
149. Ibid., pp. 145-7.
150. B. Mondin, *Gesù Cristo salvatore dell'uomo: Cristologia storica e sistematica* (Bologna: Edizioni Studio Domenicano, 1993), p. 355. 'The miracles of Jesus [...] show that the Messianic Kingdom, through which the salvific plan of God, announced by the Prophets, is fulfilled, is realised in his person' (ibid.).
151. A. Camps, *Jerome Xavier*, p. 147.
152. G. Crespi and G. Samir Eid, *L'Islam. Storia, fede, cultura* (Brescia: La Scuola, 1996), p. 175; and V. Colombo, *Sifah e Hal: Teorie dell'Unicità Divina nel pensiero Mu'Tazili-ta* (Milan: EDUCatt, 2007), p. 105.
153. A. Camps, *Jerome Xavier*, pp. 147-8.
154. Ibid., p. 143.
155. In fact, usually in the Islamic state, the sultan is also subject to Koranic law, to which the *ulama* recognize only 'the right to legislate on secular matters on which the *shariah* has gaps or inadequate regulatory prerequisites' (E. Pace, *Islam e Occidente* [Rome: Edizioni Lavoro, 1995], p. 52).

6 Conclusion

The figure of Akbar, whose personality remains one of the most fascinating and enigmatic kings of his time and of the whole of Indian history, is still the subject of wide academic debate. In particular, his religious policy is a subject on which there is profound disagreement among historians. For our study, it was necessary to address this issue, with which the subject we were interested in is closely connected. We have noted from the outset that the Jesuit missions in Mughal lands were always at the behest of a Muslim ruler—at least nominally—and such an initiative does not seem to have been found elsewhere in history. As we know, Muslims generally have no interest in learning about religions other than Islam, the *din al-fitra*, to which Christianity and Judaism are a deviation. Consequently, reading the Bible, a text that before its alteration contained in part the same Koranic message, is considered as a useless if not dangerous activity.

It is understandable that the political authorities of Goa were initially suspicious of the emperor's singular request, while the ecclesiastical side did not rule out the possibility of a new 'Constantinian shift'. Various arguments were put forward to offer an interpretation of his interest in Christianity. The missionaries themselves excluded that the emperor had considered the possibility of his conversion to Christianity. We also find it difficult to accept the hypothesis that the emperor aimed to establish a new syncretic cult, a synthesis of the different faiths with which he came in contact.

In addition to possible political reasons of not being always peaceful with the Portuguese, scholars have sometimes emphasized the cosmopolitan spirit of the emperor, which was incompatible with attachment to a particular culture. He is described as an enlightened ruler who liked to surround himself with artists, men of letters and philosophers of different geographical origins. So he wanted to get in touch with some exponents of Christian thought, who could also contribute to the activities of the *Maktab Khana*. This assumption, while valid, seems to us to simplify the complexity of the issue.

Akbar would certainly never have publicly expressed his intention to renounce Islam, a move he knew had the potential to jeopardize his throne. Indeed, he was officially declaring his intention to rule in the name of a Muslim theocracy. However, it is certain that the Great Mughal gradually assumed positions that broke with Sunni orthodoxy. Often scholars who support Akbar's apostasy consider Islam as a monolith and disregard its internal divisions, identifying it only with Sunnism. We have seen how the emperor—despite his interest in the different religious systems and Islamic currents considered to be heterodox—always remained within the framework of Islam, orienting himself above all towards a Sufic spirituality.

Akbar's religious policy seems to be the fruit of a shrewd reflection, certainly and prevalently provoked by motivations of reason of state, but also on the basis of his own religious convictions. The implementation of a policy inspired by the Sufic principle of *Sulh-i-kul*, to be recognized as the sovereign by all his subjects irrespective of their adherence to faith, represented the only way to definitively consolidate his power in a country where the Mughals were, after all, foreigners in their homeland and in their faith. The promulgation of a series of measures, culminating in the recognition and protection of the right to religious freedom—with the consequent risk of undermining the superior status of Islam—only provoked the indignant reaction of those who had always held religious powers and privileges. It was therefore necessary for the sovereign to free himself from any religious control, especially that exercised by the Sunni *ulama*, those who claimed to have a monopoly on the interpretation of the *Shari'a*, to which the sultan was also subject. The emperor, therefore, exerted a great deal of pressure to grant him the title of Caliph and the consequent power to legislate in religious matters.

At this point, it could have been more convenient for Akbar to claim a prophetic role, equating himself with, or even arrogating to himself, a certain superiority over Muhammad: a condition which would have allowed him not only to be definitively relieved of all religious control, but to exercise religious power itself. Such an objective could be achieved through the disavowal of the truthful claim of Koranic revelation that establishes Muhammad as the last prophet. As we have seen, the emperor was not interested in arguments in favour of Christianity, but in its effective anti-Islamic polemic. The contribution of his Jesuit guests, whose rational demonstrations of the superiority of Jesus over Muhammad undermined his status as the 'seal of prophecy', was fundamental. Therefore, after him, God was free to raise up other prophet-legislators, such as Akbar himself.

At the same time, imperial propaganda emphasized the figure of the sovereign and underlined how he had been the object of a particular divine predilection, going so far as to identify him with the Perfect (or Universal) Man, the object of Sufic speculation. The Perfect Man is the one who has realized in himself the archetype of sublimated humanity and is filled with divine friendship, so he cannot be subject to any religious or juridical limitation. The Great Mughal, increasingly surrounded by a court devoted to him and having by now neutralized the forces of Sunnite traditionalism, soon began to exercise his claimed right to legislate also in the religious sphere.[1]

Akbar promoted a form of devotion to Jesus at the court, not as the Christ of Christianity, but as he is depicted in Sufic mysticism, where he is held in the highest esteem. He is, in fact, the prototype of the perfect teacher, as well as the 'Seal of universal holiness', as defined by Ibn Arabi. The Great Mughal, in the wake of this tradition, also elevated Christ as the model of kingship: as he well knew, he was a universal figure, potentially able to be accepted by both Muslims and Hindus. So he could not have adopted a better emblem to express his sovereignty, taking into account the effective support of the visual power of Christian iconography. In fact, the sovereign, in order to strengthen the loyalty and devotion of his closest courtiers and officials—who among other things were bearers of different spiritual sensibilities and religious beliefs—had established a circle in the palace similar to a Sufic brotherhood. It had also resorted to the images of Jesus and the Apostles present in Western devotional art to express the type of relationship that had to inspire relations within the so-called *Din-i-Ilahi.*

In the light of the above, it is clear that the presence of the Jesuits in Mughal India was, above all, functional to Akbar's wider programme of legitimizing his power. At the court, the Fathers brought arguments to demonstrate the superiority of Christianity; arguments that, in some way, proved useful to increase the personal prestige of the sovereign.

From a strictly missionary point of view, the Jesuits could certainly not show great satisfaction. At the court, the mission had obtained the maximum result that could be achieved in practice; only with regard to the local population could further developments be envisaged, although at the time there were few conversions, mainly among the 'outcast' Hindus. It was a question of laying the foundations for a long-term work, leaving the joy of the harvest to others, but subsequent geopolitical developments thwarted all hopes. On the other hand, from the cultural point of view, the mission produced considerable effects in Mughal figurative art, with the result of allowing the creation of the first Christian literature in Persian.

NOTE

1. A number of legislative measures can be mentioned, such as the non-compulsory circumcision, the abolition of the Muslim calendar in favour of the solar calendar, religious freedom extended to all faiths, permission to trade wine, the promotion of Koranic studies and a liturgy in Persian, etc. (M.L. Roy Choudhury, *The Din-i-Ilahi or the Religion of Akbar*, pp. 140-71).

Bibliography

SOURCES

Abu'l-Fadl, *Ain-i-Akbari*, vol. I (Calcutta: G.M. Rouse, 1873).

———, *Akbarnama*, vol. III (Delhi: Low Price Publications, 2007).

Bada'uni, *Muntakhab al-Tawarikh*, vol. II (New Delhi: Saeed International, 1990).

Camps, A. (ed.), 'An Unpublished Letter of Father Christoval de Vega S.J.', in id., *Studies in Asian Mission History* (Leiden: Brill Academic Publishers, 2000).

Correla-Afonso, J. (ed.), *Letters from the Mughal Court: The First Jesuit Mission to Akbar, 1580-1583* (Mumbai: Heras Institute of Indian History and Culture, 1980).

Haidar, M. (ed.), *Mukatabat-i-Al-lami [Insha-i-Abul Fazl]* (New Delhi: Munshiram Manoharlal, 1998).

Hosten, H. (ed.), 'Father A. Monserrate's Account of Akbar', *Journal of Asiatic Society of Bengal*, vol. 8, no. 5 (1912), pp. 185-221.

Hoyland, J.S. and S.N. Banerjee (eds), *The Commentary of Father Monserrate, S.J., on His Journey to the Court of Akbar* (Oxford: Oxford University Press, 1922).

Peruschi, G., *Informatione del Regno e stato del gran Rè di Mogor* (Brescia: P.M. Marchetti, 1597).

Wicki, J. (ed.), *Documenta Indica*, vols XII, XV-XVIII (Rome: Institutum Historicum Societatis Iesu, 1972-88).

Xavier, J., *Fuente de Vida. Tratado Apologético dirigido al Rey Mogol de la India en 1600* (San Sebastian: Universidad de Duesto, 2007).

———, *Mir'at al-quds (Mirror of Holiness): A Life of Christ for Emperor Akbar* (Leiden: Brill, 2012).

REFERENCES

Abd el-Jalil, J.M., *Testimone del Corano e del Vangelo* (Milan: Jaca Book, 2006).

Addas, C., *Ibn Arabi ou la quète du soufre rouge* (Paris: Gallimard, 1989).

Agrawal, A., *Studies in Mughal History* (Delhi: Motilal Banarsidass, 1983).

Al-Faruqi, I.R., *Islam and Other Faiths* (Leicester: Islamic Foundation, 1998).

Amaladass, G. and G. Lowner, *Christian Themes in Indian Art: From the Mogul Times till Today* (New Delhi: Manohar, 2012).

Aneer, G., *Akbar the Great Mogul and his Religious Thoughts* (Uppsala: Skriv Service AB, 1973).

Athar, Ali M., *Mughal India: Studies in Polity, Ideas, Society, and Culture* (New Delhi: Oxford University Press, 2006).

Azzi, J., *Le Prétre et le Prophéte. Aux sources du Coran* (Paris: M&L, 2004).

Bailey, G.A., *Art on the Jesuit Missions in Asia and Latin America, 1542-1773* (Toronto: University of Toronto Press, 1999).

———, 'The Indian Conquest of Catholic Art: The Mughals, the Jesuits, and Imperial Mural Painting', *Art Journal*, vol. 57, no. 1 (1998), pp. 24-30.

———, *The Jesuits and the Grand Mogul: Renaissance Art at the Imperial Court of India, 1580-1630* (Washington: Smithsonian Institution, 1998).

———, 'The Truth-Showing Mirror: Jesuit Catechism and the Arts in Mughal India', in J.W. O'Malley, G.A. Bailey, S.J. Harris and T.F. Kennedy (eds), *The Jesuits: Cultures, Sciences, and the Arts, 1540-1773* (Toronto: University of Toronto Press, 1999), pp. 381-401.

Baldussi, A., 'Dalla periferia al centro', in A. Baldussi, P. Manduchi and N. Melis (eds), *Le mille e una strada. Viaggiare pellegrini nel mondo musulmano* (Milan: Franco Angeli, 2005), pp. 113-242.

Barocchi, P. *Trattati d'arte del Cinquecento*, vol. II (Bari: G. Laterza, 1961).

Bartoli, D., *Missione al Gran Mogòr* (Rome: Salerno Editrice, 1998).

Bearman, P.J., T. Bianquis, C.E. Bosworth, E. Van Donzel and W.P. Heinrichs (eds), *Encyclopédie de l'Islam*, vol. II (Leiden: Brill, 1960).

Besançon, A., *L'image interdite. Une histoire intellectuelle de l'iconoclasme* (Paris: Fayard, 1994).

Behr, H., *I moghul: Imperatori dell'India* (Milan: Garzanti, 1985).

Bishop, G., *In Search of Cathay: The Travels of Bento de Goes, S.J. (1562-1607)* (Anand: Gujarat Sahitya Prakash, 1998).

Boespflug, F., *Dieu et ses images. Une histoire de l'éternel dans l'art* (Paris: Bayard, 2008).

Boyajian, J.C., *Portuguese Trade in Asia Under the Habsburgs, 1580-1640* (Baltimore: Johns Hopkins University Press, 2007).

Branca, P., *Pagine di letteratura araba* (Milan: EDUCatt, 2009).

Buckler, F.W., 'A New Interpretation of Akbar's Infallibility Decree of 1579', *Journal of the Royal Asiatic Society*, vol. 10 (1924), pp. 591-608.

Burke, S.M., *Akbar: The Greatest Mogul* (New Delhi: Munshiram Manoharlal, 1989).

Calza, G.C., 'Akbar: Il più grande', id. (ed.), *Akbar*, pp. 13-20.

Camps, A., *Jerome Xavier S.J. and the Muslims of the Mogul Empire: Controversial Works and Missionary Activity* (Schoneck-Beckenried: Nouvelle Revue de Science Missionnaire, 1957).

———, *Studies in Asian Mission History* (Leiden: Brill Academic Publishers, 2000).

Carvalho, P.M., '"Rarities from Goa" at the Courts of Humayun, Akbar and Jahangir (1530-1627)', in J. Flores and N. Vassallo e Silva (eds), *Goa and the Great Mughal* (Lisbon: Calouste Gulbenkian Foundation, 2004), pp. 98-115.

Casadei, M., 'La Siria, terra di missione nella Didascalia di Addai: Il viaggio e l'apostolo', *Quaderni di storia religiosa*, vol. 13 (2006), pp. 95-116.

Cellini, P., *La Madonna di S. Luca in S. Maria Maggiore* (Rome: Instituto Grafico Tiberino, 1943).

Chaurasia, R.S., *History of Medieval India: From 1000 A.D. to 1707 A.D.* (New Delhi: Atlantic, 2002).

Chodkiewicz, M., *Le Sceau des Saints, Prophétie et Sainteté dans la doctrine d'Ibn 'Arabî* (Paris: Gallimard, 1986).

Cimino, R.M., 'Un missionario italiano alla corte dei "Mogor": il Padre Francesco Corsi', in E. Fasana and G. Sorge (eds), *Civiltà indiana ed impatto europeo nei secoli XVI-XVIII: L'apporto dei viaggiatori e missionari italiani* (Milan: Jaca Book, 1987), pp. 201-22.

Clot, A., *Les grands moghols: Splendeur et chute* (Paris: Plon, 1993).

Clothey, F.W., *Religion in India: A Historical Introduction* (Abingdon: Routledge, 2006).

Cocozza, D., *Cristo: Un profeta tra Bibbia e Corano* (Rome: Editoria scientifica, 2008).

Colombo, E., *Convertire i musulmani. L'esperienza di un gesuita spagnolo del Seicento* (Turin: Bruno Mondadori, 2007).

———, 'Jesuits and Islam in Seventeenth-Century Europe: War, Preaching and Conversions', in B. Heyberger, M. Garcia-Arenal, E. Colombo and P. Vismara (eds), *L'Islam visto da Occidente: Cultura e religione del Seicento europeo di fronte all'Islam* (Genoa-Milan: Marietti, 2009), pp. 315-40.

———, 'Gesuitomania: Studi recenti sulle missioni gesuitiche (1540-1773)', in M. Catto, G. Mongini and S. Mostaccio (eds), *Evangelizzazione e Globalizzazione: Le missioni gesuitiche nell'età moderna tra storia e storiografia* (Rome: Società Editrice Dante Alighieri, 2010).

Colombo, V., *Sifah e Hal: Teorie dell'Unicità Divina nel pensiero Mu'Tazili-ta* (Milan: EDUCatt, 2007).

Correia-Afonso, J., 'The Second Jesuit Mission to Akbar', *Indica*, vol. 28 (1991), pp. 73-93.

———, *The Jesuits in India: 1542-1773* (Anand: Gujarat Sahitya Prakash, 1997).

Couto, D. do, *Da Asia*, Década Quinta, Parte segunda (Lisbon: Regia Officina Typografica, 1780).

Crespi, G. and Samir Eid G., *L'Islam. Storia, fede, cultura* (Brescia: La Scuola, 1996).

Cronin, V., *The Wise Man from the West: Matteo Ricci and His Mission to China* (London: Fount Paperbacks, 1984).

Çuturi, F. (ed.), *In nome di Dio. L'impresa missionaria di fronte all'alterità* (Rome: Meltemi, 2004).

Cuypers, M. and Gobillot G., *Le Coran* (Paris: Le Cavalier Bleu, 2007).

D'Ascia, L., *Il Corano e la tiara. L'epistola a Maometto di Enea Silvio Piccolomini (papa Pio II)* (Bologne: Pendragon, 2001).

De Filippo, G., *Beato Rodolfo Acquaviva S.J.* (Teramo: Edigrafital, 1999).

Debergh, M., 'Premiers jalons de l'évangélisation de l'Inde, du Japon et de la Chine', in J.M. Mayeur, C. Pietri, A. Vauchez and M. Venard (eds), *Histoire du Christianisme*, vol. VIII: *Le temps des confessions (1530-1620)* (Paris: Desclée, 1992), pp. 787-853.

Delmaire, J.M. and N.M. Zakka, *Jésus dans la littérature arabe et hébraique contemporaine* (Villeneuve d'Ascq: Presses universitaires du Septentrion, 1998).

Devapriam, E., 'Repercussions of the Counter-Reformation on the Works of the Mughal and the Florentine Painters' Realism in the Late Sixteenth and Early Seventeenth Centuries', in D. Jones (ed.), *A Mirror of Princes: The Mughals and the Medici* (Mumbai: Marg Publications, 1987), pp. 151-7.

Di Noia, A.M., *Maometto* (Rome: Newton Compton, 2012).

Didier, H., *Fantomes d'Islam et de Chine. Le voyage de Bento de Gois S.J. (1603-1607)* (Paris: Chandeigne, 2003).

_______, 'Le non publié et l'impubliable: le cas des Jésuites missionaries en terre d'Islam, XVIe-XVIIIe siècles', *Transversalités: Revue de l'Institut catholique de Paris* (July-September 2007), pp. 15-25.

_______, 'Muslim Heterodoxy, Persian Murtaddun and Jesuit Missionaries at the Court of King Akbar (1580-1605)', *The Heythrop Journal*, vol. 49, no. 6 (2008), pp. 898-939.

_______, 'Ormuz, point d'appui de la mission des Jésuites auprès du Roy Akbar (années 1580-1605)', in D. Couto and R.M. Loureiro (eds), *Revisiting Hormuz: Portuguese Interactions in the Persian Gulf Region in the Early Modern Period* (Wiesbaden: Otto Harrassowitz GmbH & Co.KG, 2008), pp. 163-76.

_______, 'Jérome Xavier, conseiller chrétien d'Akbar (1542-1605), roi aussi machiavélique que musulman?', in M.T. Urvoy (ed.), *Islam et christianisme. Éthique et politique* (Éditions de Paris, 2010), pp. 103-41.

_______, 'Jérome Xavier, critique de l'éthique musulmane dans Fuente de Vida, au nom de la dignité de la femme', in M.T. Urvoy (ed.), *Christianisme et islam. Foi et Loi* (Versailles: Éditions de Paris, 2010), pp. 71-98.

_______, 'Les jésuites auprès du Grand Mogol Akbar (fin xvie siècle): une mission chrétienne atypique auprès d'un souvrain musulman atypique?', in B. Heyberger and R. Madinier (eds), *L'Islam des marges: mission chrétienne et espaces périphériques du monde musulman XVI-XXe siècles* (Paris: Karthala, 2011), p. 17.

_______, 'Jerónimo Javier, un navarro en la India', in V. Maurya and M. Insua (eds), *Actas del I Congreso Ibero-Asiatico de Hispanistas Siglo de Oro e Hispanismo General* (Pamplona: Universidad de Navarra, 2011), pp. 147-58.

_______, 'Le role de l'iconographie dans les missions jésuites (Inde du nord et Tibet, XVIe-XVIIe siècles)', in J. Pirotte, C. Sappia and O. Servais (eds), *Images et diffusion du christianisme. Expressions graphiques en contexte missionnaire XVIe-XXe siècles* (Lyon: Karthala, 2012), pp. 45-56.

Dousse, M., *Maria la musulmana. Importanza e significato della madre del Messia nel Corano* (Rome: Arkeios, 2006).

Eraly, A., *The Last Spring: The Lives and Times of the Great Mughals* (New Delhi: Viking, 1997).

———, *Emperors of the Peacock Throne: The Saga of the Great Mughals* (London: Penguin Books, 2001).

———, *The Mughal Throne: The Saga of India's Great Emperors* (London: W&N, 2004).

Étèvenaux, J., *Histoire des missions chrétiennes* (Saint-Maurice: Saint-Augustin, 2004).

Ettinghausen, R., *La peinture arabe* (Geneva: Skira, 1962).

Fasana, E., 'Introduzione', in E. Fasana and G. Sorge (eds), *India tra Oriente e Occidente. L'apporto dei viaggiatori e missionari italiani nei secoli XVI-XVIII* (Milan: Jaca Book, 199); pp. 7-22.

Flores, J. and A. Vasconcelos de Saldanha, *Os Firangis na chancelaria mogul: Cópias Portuguesas de documentos de Akbar (1572-1604)* (New Delhi: Embaixada de Portugal, 2003).

Fortunati, Pietrantonio V., *La Pittura in Emilia e in Romagna*, I. *Il Cinquecento: un'avventura artistica tra natura e idea* (Bologna: Nuova Alfa, 1994).

Frédéric, L., *Le tigre et la rose. Une passion à la cour des Grands Moghols* (Paris: Robert Laffont, 1984).

———, *Akbar le Grand Moghol* (Paris: Denoel, 1986).

———, *L'Inde de l'IsIàm* (Paris: Arthaud, 1989).

Gaborieau, M., 'Akbar et la construction de l'empire (1556-1605)', in C. Markovits (ed.), *Histoire dell'Inde moderne, 1480-1950* (Lille: Fayard, 1994), pp. 97-114.

Gallo, M., *Omelia arabocristiana dell'VIII secolo* (Rome: Città Nuova, 1994).

Gnilka, J., *Bibbia e Corano* (Milan: Àncora, 2006).

———, *Die Nazarener und der Koran. Eine Spurensuche* (Freiburg im Breisgau: Herder Verlag Gmbh, 2007).

Goggi, R., 'Introduzione alla Questione 4', in San Tommaso d'Aquino, *Le questioni disputate*, I (Bologna: Edizioni Studio Domenicano, 1992).

Goldie, F., *First Christian Mission to the Great Mogul* (Dublin: M.H. Gill and Son, 1897).

Gregorovius, F., *Storia di Roma nel Medioevo* (Rome: Einaudi, 1966).

Guarducci, M., *La più antica icona di Maria: un prodigioso vincolo fra Oriente e Occidente* (Rome: Ist. Poligrafico dello Stato, 1989).

Gulbenkian, R., 'Os quatro Evangelhos em persa da Biblioteca Nacional de Lisboa, o Grào Mongol, os Jesmtas e os Arménios', *Anais da Academia Portuguesa de História*, II Série, vol. XXV (Lisbon: Academia Portuguesa da História, 1969).

Gupta, M.L., *Sources of Mughal History, 1526 to 1740* (New Delhi: Atlantic, 1989).

Guzman, I. de, *Historia de las missiones que han hecho los religiosos de la Compunta de Iesus para predicar el Sancto Evangelio en la India Orientai, y en los Reynos de la China y Iapon,* vol. III (Alcala: Viuda de Juan Gracián, 1601).

Hanggi, H., 'Come gli Indù vedono Gesù Cristo', *Communio: Rivista internazionale di Teologia e Cultura*, vol. 213 (2007), pp. 29-39.

Hasan, M., *Sayyid Abul A'Ala Maududi and His Thought*, vol. I (Lahore: Islamic Publications, 1984).

Habib, I., 'Introduction: Commemorating Akbar', in I.A. Khan (ed.), *Akbar and His Age* (Delhi: Northern Book Centre, 1999), pp. xi-xvi.

Hay, I., *De rebus japonicis, indicis et peruanis epistolae recentiores* (Anversa: 1605).

Hambye, E.R., 'The First Jesuit Mission to Emperor Akbar', in C.W. Troll (ed.), *Islam in India: Studies and Commentaries*, vol. I (New Delhi: Vikas Publishing House, 1982), pp. 3-13.

Jackson, P., 'Christian–Muslim Dialogue in India', *Studia Missionalia*, vol. XLIII (Rome: Pontificia Università Gregoriana, 1994), pp. 159-76.

Jahan, I., *Socio-Cultural Life in Medieval History* (Solapur: Laxmi Book Publication, 2018).

Jarric, P. du, *Histoire des choses plus mémorables advenues tant* és *Indes Orientale qu'autres pays de la descouverte des Portugais en l'establissement et progrez de la foy Chrestienne et Catholique*, vol. I (Bordeaux: S. Millanges, 1610).

———, *Akbar and the Jesuits: An Account of the Jesuit Missions to the Court of Akbar* (London: 1926).

Junghare, I.A., *Topics in Pali Historical Phonology* (Delhi: Motilal Banarsidass, 2008).

Khan, I.A., 'Akbar's Personality Traits and World Outlook: A Critical Reappraisal', in I. Habib (ed.), *Akbar and His India* (New Delhi: Oxford University Press, 1997).

Koch, E., 'The Influence of the Jesuit Mission on Symbolic Representations of the Mughal Emperors', in C.W. Troll (ed.), *Islam in India*, pp. 14-32.

———, 'Pietre Dure and Other Artistic Contacts between the Court of the Mughals and that of the Medici', in D. Jones (ed.), *A Mirror of Princes*, pp. 29-56.

Lê Thành, K., *Islam: La storia, le istituzioni, le differenze culturali* (Rome: Armando Editore, 2001).

Lécrivain, P., '"Cherchant le Cathay, il trouva le Ciel...": Bento de Góis

S-J. en Asie Centrale (1602-1607)', *Transversalités* (April-June 2012), pp. 13-27.

MacLagan, E., *The Jesuits and the Great Mogul* (New York: Octagon Books, 1972).

Madhok, P., 'Christian–Islamic Relations in the Court Art of Mughal Indian', *The International Journal of the Arts in Society*, vol. 4 (2010), pp. 1-16.

Majorana, B., 'Tra carità e cultura. Formazione e prassi missionaria nella Compagnia di Gesù', in P. Broggio, F. Cantù, P.A. Fabre and A. Romano (eds), *I gesuiti ai tempi di Claudio Acquaviva: Strategie politiche, religiose e culturali tra Cinque e Seicento* (Brescia: Morcelliana, 2007), pp. 226-31.

Malekandathil, P., *Trade, Religion and Polity in the Indian Ocean* (Delhi: Primus Books, 2010).

Malik, M., *History of India* (New Delhi: New Saraswati House, 2016).

Margolin, C., *Neuf années de bibliographie érasmienne, 1962-1970* (Paris: Vrin, 1977).

Mariotti, A., 'La prima missione dei Gesuiti alla corte di Akbar', in E. Fasana and G. Sorge (eds), *India tra Oriente e Occidente* (Milan: Jaca Book, 1991), pp. 75-100.

Marzolo, P., 'Saggio sui segni', in *Annali delle Università toscane* (Pisa: 1867), pp. 53-129.

Mathew, K.S., 'Akbar and the Europeans: A Study of Changing Perspectives', in I.A. Khan (ed.), *Akbar and His Age*, pp. 114-31.

________, *Portuguese and the Sultanate of Gujarat* (Delhi: Mittal Publications, 1986).

Matringe, D., *Un Islam non arabe. Horizons indiens et pakistanais* (Paris: Téraèdre, 2005).

Mervin, S., *L'Islam. Fondamenti e dottrine* (Milan: Pearson Italia, 2004).

Metha, J.L., *Advanced Study in the History of Medieval India*, vol. II (New Delhi: Sterling Publishers, 1986).

Milanetti, G., 'Religione e religioni alla corte di Akbar', in G.C. Calza (ed.), *Akbar* (Rome: Skira, 2012), pp. 52-9.

Mondin, B., *Gesù Cristo salvatore dell'uomo. Cristologia storica e sistematica* (Bologna: Edizioni Studio Domenicano, 1993).

Moosvi, S., 'The Road to Suhl-i Kul: Akbar's Alienation from Theological Islam', in I. Habib (ed.), *Religion in Indian History* (New Delhi: Tulika Books), 2010, pp. 167-76.

Moubarak, Y., *Recherches sur la pensée chrétienne et l'Islam dans les temps modernes et à l'époque contemporaine* (Beirut: Université libanaise, 1977).

Narayan, J.S., *Acquaviva and the Great Mogul* (Patna: Catholic Book Club, 1945).

Nastri, G.G., *Libertà della fede. Necessità della ragione. Costruzione della filosofia al di là dell'influenza cartesiana protestante* (Rome: Armando Editore, 2009).

Neil, S., *A History of Christianity in India*, vol. I: *The Beginnings to AD 1707* (Cambridge: Cambridge University Press, 1984).

Newitt, M., *A History of Portuguese Overseas Expansion 1400-1668* (London: Routledge, 2004).

Nizami, K.A., *Akbar and Religion* (Delhi: Idarah-i-Adabiyat-i-Delli, 1989).

Noer, F.C.K.A. von, *The Emperor Akbar: A Contribution Towards the History of India in the 16th Century*, vol. I (Calcutta: Thacker, Spink & Company, 1890).

Okada, A., *Le Grand Moghol et ses peintres* (Paris: Flammarion, 1992).

Oliveira, Lopes R., *Arte e Alteridade. Confluencias da Arte Cristà na India, na China e no Japào, séc. XVI a XVIII*, Ph.D. thesis in Fine Arts (Lisbon: University of Lisbon, 2011).

O'Neill, C.E. and J.M. Dominguez (eds), *Diccionario histórico de la Compania de Jesùs.* Biogràfico-Temàtico, vol. IV (Roma-Madrid: University Pontifica Comillas, 2001).

Pace, E., *Islam e Occidente* (Rome: Edizioni Lavoro, 1995).

Palumbo, G., 'La verità disputata: la missione di Rodolfo Acquaviva alla corte di Akbar tra passione per la parola e sfiducia nei miracoli', in C. Lavarra (ed.), *La linea Acquaviva: Dal nepotismo rinascimentale al meriggio della Riforma Cattolica* (Conversano: Mario Congedo, 2005), pp. 49-75.

Pellicani, I., *I Rajput. Storia, leggende e tradizioni dei Samurai dell'India* (Roma: Newton Compton, 1994).

Prémare, A.L. de, *Les fondations de l'Islam. Entre écriture et histoire* (Paris: Seuil, 2002).

Rahman, S.A., *Punishment of Apostasy in Islam* (Selangor: The Other Press Sdn Bhd).

Ravier, A., *Ignatius of Loyola and the Founding of the Society of Jesus* (San Francisco: Ignatius Press, 1987).

Ricci, M., *Della entrata della Compagnia di Giesù e Christianità nella Cina* (Macerata: Quodlibet, 2000).

Richards, J.F., *The Mughal Empire* (Cambridge University Press, 1993).

Ringgenberg, P., *L'univers symbolique des arts islamiques* (Paris: L'Harmattan, 2009).

Rizvi, S.A.A., *Religious and Intellectual History of the Muslims in Akbar's Reign with Special Reference to Abu'l Fazl (1556-1606)* (New Delhi: Munshiram Manoharlal, 1975).

———, 'Dimensions of Sulh-i Kul (Universal Peace) in Akbar's Reign and the Sufi Theory of Perfect Man', in I.A Khan (ed.), *Akbar and His Age*, pp. 3-22.

Rizvi, S.A.A. and V.J. Adams Flynn, *Fatehpur Sikri* (Mumbai: D.B. Taraporevala Sons, 1975).

Rizzi, M., *Le prime traduzioni del Corano in Italia* (Turin: L'Harmattan Italia, 2007).

Rooney, J., *The Hesitant Dawn: Christianity in Pakistan* (Rawalpindi: Christian Study Centre, 1984).

Roy Choudhury, M.L., *The Din-i-Ilahi or the Religion of Akbar* (New Delhi: Munshiram Manoharlal, 1952).

Saaidia, O., 'L'évangélisation des musulmans, mission impossible?', in J. Pirotte (ed.), *Résistances à l'évangélisation. Interprétations historiques et enjeux théologiques* (Paris: Karthala, 2004), pp. 257-71.

Saccone, C., *I percorsi dell'Islam. Dall'esilio di Ismaele alla rivolta dei nostri giorni* (Padua: Messaggero, 2003).

Santos, Hernandez A.S., 'Dos Javieres en la India', *Miscelanea Comillas*, vol. 10, no. 18 (1952), pp. 33-87.

———, *Jeronimo Javier S.J., apostol del Gran Mogol y arzobispo electo de Cranganor, en la India* (Pamplona: Editorial Gómez, 1958).

Schweitzer, A., *The Quest of the Historical Jesus* (North Chelmsford: Courier Corporation, 2012).

Sen, A., 'East and West: The Reach of Reason', in T. Bentley and D.S. Jones (eds), *The Moral Universe* (London: Demos, 2001), pp. 19-33.

———, *The Argumentative Indian: Writings on Indian History* (London: Penguin, 2006).

Sharma, S.R., *The Religious Policy of the Mughal Emperors* (New Delhi: Munshiram Manoharlal, 1988).

Silva, Rego A. da, *Le Patronage portugais de l'Orient* (Agencia Geral do Ultramar, 1957).

Skali, F., *Gesù nella tradizione sufi* (Milan: Paoline, 2007).

Smith, V.A., *Akbar the Great Mogul* (Delhi: S. Chand & Co., 1962).

Srivastava, A.L., *A Short History of Akbar the Great (1542-1605)* (Agra: Shiva Lal Agarwala, 1957).

Stronge, S., 'Il Libro di Akbar (Akbarnama) e la cultura di corte in epoca moghul', in G.C. Calza (ed.), *Akbar*, pp. 21-9.

Suau, P., *Les bienheureux martyrs de Salsette. Rodolphe d'Acquaviva et ses compagnons de la Compagnie de Jesus* (Lille: Société de Saint-Augustin, 1893).

Subrahmanyam, S., *The Portuguese Empire in Asia: 1500-1700* (Hoboken: Wiley-Blackwell, 2012).

Surme, S.A., *Kurdistan: Storia, economia e risorse, società e tradizioni, arte e cultura, religione* (Bologna: Pendragon, 1998).

Thekkedath, J., *History of Christianity in India*, II (Bangalore: Church History Association of India, 2001).

Torri, M., *Storia dell'India* (Laterza: Bari, 2000).

Toscano, G.M., *Alla scoperta del Tibet* (Bologna: EMI, 1977).

Tramontana, S., 'Comunicare nel Mezzogiorno', in G. Musca and V. Sivo (eds), *Strumenti, tempi e luoghi di comunicazione nel Mezzogiorno normanno-svevo* (Bari: Dedalo, 1995), pp. 9-30.

Troll, C.W., *Domande islamiche. Risposte ristiane* (Brescia: Queriniana, 2010).

Tucci, G., *Italia e Oriente* (Rome: ISAIO, 2005).

Vassallo e Silva, N., 'Precious Stones, Jewels and Cameos: Jacques de Coutre's Journey to Goa and Agra', in J. Flores and N. Vassallo e Silva (eds), *Goa and the Great Mughal* (Lisbon: Calouste Gulebenkian Foundation, 2004).

Vismara, P., 'Il cattolicesimo dalla "riforma cattolica" all'assolutismo', in G. Filoramo and D. Menozzi (eds), *Storia del cristianesimo,* III, *L'età moderna* (Bari: Laterza, 1997).

Waraich, S., 'Competing and Complementary Visions of the Court of the Great Mogor', in D. Leibsohn and J. Favrot Peterson (eds), *Seeing Across Cultures in the Early Modern World* (Farnham: Ashgate, 2012), pp. 73-94.

Watt, W.M., *Muslim–Christian Encounters: Perceptions and Misperceptions* (London: Routledge, 2013).

Wellez, E., *Akbar's Religious Thought Reflected in Mogul Painting* (London: George Allen and Unwin, 1952).

Wessel, C., *Early Jesuit Travellers in Central Asia* (Delhi: Low Price Publications, 1999).

Zupanov, I.G., 'Correnti e controcorrenti. La geopolitica gesuita in Asia (XVI secolo)', in P. Broggio, F. Cantù, P.A. Fabre and A. Romano (eds), *I gesuiti ai tempi di Claudio Acquaviva* (Brescia: Morcelliana, 2007).

Index

PLATES

Plate 1. Anonymous, *Jesus and the Arrogant Hermit.*

Plate 2. Anonymous, *The Ascension of Jesus.*

Plate 3. Pieter van der Borcht, *Pietatis Concordiæ.*

Plate 4. Govardhan, *Akbar with a Lion and a Lamb.*

Plate 5. Pieter van der Borcht, *Pietas Regia.*

Plate 6. Basawan, *Madonna and Child.*

Plate 7. Hashim e Abu'l Hasan, *Jahangir and Jesus.*

Plate 8. Anonymous, *Madonna del Popolo.*

Plate 9. Salim Quli, *Jesus Asleep During a Storm at Sea.*

Plate 10. Representation of Lord Vishnu.

Plate 11. Vishnu on Snake Ananta.